The

Quotable

Kennedy

edited by **ALEX J. GOLDMAN**

THE CITADEL PRESS
NEW YORK

Contents

CONTENTS

Acknowledgments

For permission to quote, the author acknowledges with thanks the following:

ANTI-DEFAMATION LEAGUE OF B'NAI B'RITH, New York, for *A Nation of Immigrants,* by John F. Kennedy.

ATHENEUM PUBLISHERS, New York, for *John F. Kennedy, President,* by Hugh Sidey. Copyright © 1963, 1964 by Hugh Sidey.

COUNTRY BEAUTIFUL FOUNDATION, INC., Waukesha, Wisconsin, for *America the Beautiful in the Words of John F. Kennedy,* Copyright © 1963 by the Country Beautiful Foundation, Inc.

WILFRED FUNK, INC., New York, for *Why England Slept,* by John F. Kennedy.

HARPER & ROW, INC., New York, for *Profiles in Courage,* by John F. Kennedy, and *The Strategy of Peace,* by John F. Kennedy.

THE RIDGE PRESS, INC., New York, for "The Arts in America," from *Creative America.*

[7]

Preface

John Fitzgerald Kennedy has been described in many ways, usually in the most ecstatic superlatives. He was a loving son, devoted father, adoring husband, brilliant speaker, master wit, assiduous reader. He was a man of peace and a builder of men. All these descriptions are true, for John Kennedy was as remarkable a man as he was an unusual President. Every aspect of life, as it revolved around him, excited his zest and commanded his imagination.

Beyond this, John Kennedy stamped wisdom on history and on the minds of men. His wit amused and disarmed, and endeared him to millions. But his historical greatness will be largely judged by his carefully chosen words and thoughts, which have affected and inspired millions. With their stinging import and incisive penetration, they will live on, to be repeated and recalled by generations to come.

Every Kennedy phrase, seriously thought-through and weighed for truth and effect, carries tremendous implications. Each expression breathes its author's idealism and imagination. Each word reveals the studious mind. And the words, phrases, and passages as a whole reflect a wisdom and sagacity far beyond what might be expected of one of John Kennedy's actual years. Indeed, this youthful leader was a veritable "father of wisdom," to borrow from the biblical word *abrech*. This was the term applied by the ancient Egyptians to Joseph when *Pharaoh* appointed him his viceroy and gave him power over Egypt. The people escorted his chariot through the streets, crying out before him, "Abrech!"—which means "father of wisdom, though tender of age."

Presidents of the United States are often recalled by the phrases they coined. "To bigotry, no sanction" calls up George Washington. "Four score and seven years ago" brings to mind the Great Emancipator. "Make the world safe for democracy" means Woodrow Wilson. "The only thing we have to fear is fear itself" instantly brings before us the image of Franklin D. Roosevelt, with the long cigarette protruding from the longer cigarette holder. And who does not know at once the author of the statement that begins: "Ask not . . ."—or of that other, "Let the word go forth . . ."?

John F. Kennedy, like all great Presidents, was marked for the attention of posterity by his words alone. Ever the discerning reader of the great masters, thinkers, and leaders who had gone before him, Kennedy's quick, keen mind was blessed with the ability to choose the right word for the right time.

Many of his most brilliant sayings, passages, and comments have been lost in the innumerable major addresses and speeches he made before the Congress and in other parts of the world. The present writer has drawn these out, often out of context, to bring them together in this volume, where the special quality of each can be fully appreciated. Adults, students, and children who will wish to speak of, or write about and quote John Kennedy will find here many of his most stirring and meaningful comments, indexed by subject matter.

They deserve to be considered and remembered, as a testimony to John F. Kennedy's inestimable contribution to America and the world.

ALEX J. GOLDMAN

The Quotable Kennedy

Action

Action and foresight are the only possible preludes to freedom.

Senate Address
August 21, 1957

To sound the alarm is not to panic but to seek action from an aroused public. For, as the poet Dante once said: "The hottest places in hell are reserved for those who, in a time of great moral crisis, maintain their neutrality."

Foreign policy is neither successfully made nor successfully carried out by mere pronouncements. . . .

Tulsa, Oklahoma
September 16, 1959

There are no magic policies of liberation—there is only hard work—but that hard work can and must be done.

Pulaski Day Dinner
Milwaukee, Wisconsin
October 17, 1959

It is time to stop reacting to our adversary's moves, and to start acting like the bold, hopeful, inventive people that we were born to be, ready to build and begin anew, ready to make a reality of man's oldest dream, world peace.

Washington, D.C.
December 11, 1959

The American, by nature, is optimistic. He is experimental, an inventor and a builder who builds best when called upon to build greatly. Arouse his will to believe in himself, give him a great goal to believe in, and he will create the means to reach it.

Washington, D.C.
January 1, 1960

On the Presidential coat of arms, the American eagle holds in his right talon the olive branch, while in his left he holds a bundle of arrows. We intend to give equal attention to both.

State of the Union Message
January 30, 1961

Any potential aggressor contemplating an attack on any part of the free world with any kind of weapons, conventional or nuclear, must know that our response will be suitable, selective, swift and effective.

Message to Congress
March 28, 1961

The history of this nation is a tribute to the ability of an informed citizenry to make the right choices in response to danger.

Annual Convention of the
National Association of Broadcasters
May 5, 1961

There is no point in calling for vigorous action to protect our security if we are unwilling to pay the price and carry the burdens which are necessary to maintain that security.

> National Conference on
> International Economic and Social
> Development
> June 16, 1961

The hour of decision has arrived. We cannot afford to "wait and see what happens" while the tide of events sweeps over and beyond us. We must use time as a tool, not as a couch.

> National Association of Manufacturers
> New York City
> December 6, 1961

The United States did not rise to greatness by waiting for others to lead.

> State of the Union Message
> January 11, 1962

The greatest works of our nation's founders lay not in documents and declarations, but in creative, determined action.

Others may confine themselves to debate, discussion, and that ultimate luxury, free advice. Our responsibility is one of decision, for to govern is to choose.

> Independence Hall
> Philadelphia, Pennsylvania
> July 4, 1962

ACTION

This nation must move fast even to stand still.

We shall be judged more by what we do at home than by what we preach abroad.

If at times our actions seem to make life difficult for others, it is only because history has made life difficult for us all.

State of the Union Message
January 14, 1963

Let us go on, from words to actions . . .

Frankfurt, West Germany
June 25, 1963

History and our own conscience will judge us more harshly if we do not now make every effort to test our hopes by action . . .

Television Address
July 26, 1963

It is essential . . . that the word go forth from the United States to all who are concerned about the future of the Family of Man that we are not weary in well-doing. And I am confident, if we maintain the peace, that we shall in due season reap the kind of world we deserve and deserve the kind of world we shall have.

Protestant Council of New York City
New York City
November 8, 1963

[18]

America and Americans

Every American is now involved in the world.

University of Wisconsin
Madison, Wisconsin
June 16, 1958

Mr. Khrushchev may have known his Marx—but his Marx did not know the United States of America. This is no atrophied capitalist society, declining, splitting, failing. We do not live under a dying system, fading from the scene as feudalism faded some centuries ago.

University of Rochester
Rochester, New York
October 1, 1959

The cause of all mankind is the cause of America.

Merced, California
September 9, 1960

We are determined . . . that freedom shall survive and succeed; and whatever the peril and setbacks, we have some very large advantages. . . . first . . . we are on the side of liberty . . . second . . . we are not alone. . . . third . . . our desire for peace. Finally, our greatest asset . . . is the American people . . .

State of the Union Message
May 25, 1961

[19]

We are gratified, but we are not satisfied.

State of the Union Message
January 11, 1962

I do not believe our adversaries are tired, and I cannot believe that the United States of America . . . is fatigued.

Protestant Council of New York City
New York City
November 8, 1963

Armaments

Democracies which are fundamentally peaceful have to receive external stimuli to force them to rearm.

Why England Slept

A capacity for massive retaliation is the only answer to the threat of massive attack.

Lake Charles, Louisiana
October 16, 1959

The new and terrible dangers which man has created can only be controlled by man.

University of California
Los Angeles, California
November 2, 1959

Both sides in this fateful struggle must come to know, sooner or later, that the price of running this arms race to the end is death—for both.

I am sorry to say that there is too much point to the wisecrack that life is extinct on other planets because their scientists were more advanced than ours.

Washington, D.C.
December 11, 1959

The logic of the present arms race seems to require more of a collision course than the slow changes wrought in medieval times. In the days of the Crusades, it took months—sometimes years—of sailing by sea and marching overland for two worlds to collide. Today, the deadly missiles with hydrogen warheads are only minutes away.

Washington, D.C.
December 11, 1959

If genuine progress is made, then as tension is reduced, so will our arms.

Our arms will never be used to strike the first blow in any attack. This is not a confession of weakness, but a statement of strength.

The primary purpose of our arms is peace, not war.

Neither our strategy nor our psychology as a nation—and certainly not our economy—must become dependent upon the permanent maintenance of a large military establishment.

The basic problems facing the world today are not susceptible to a military solution.

Message to Congress
March 28, 1961

Our foremost aim is the control of force, not the pursuit of force, in a world made safe for mankind.

Television Address
March 2, 1962

The purpose of our military strength is peace. The purpose of our partnership is peace.

Naples, Italy
July 2, 1963

Art

There is a story that some years ago an interested mother wrote to a principal of a school, "Don't teach my boy poetry, he's going to run for Congress." I've never taken the view that the world of politics and the world of poetry are so far apart.

"Robert Frost: American Poet"
CBS Television Network
February 26, 1961

In our fulfillment of . . . responsibilities toward the arts lies our unique achievement as a free society.

Art is the great democrat, calling forth creative genius from every sector of society, disregarding race or religion or wealth or color.

Closed Circuit Television
The National Cultural Center
Washington, D.C.
November 29, 1962

We recognize increasingly the essentiality of artistic achievement. This is part . . . of a nationwide movement toward excellence. . . . It is part, too, of a feeling that art is the great unifying and humanizing experience . . . the side of life which expresses the emotions and embodies values and ideals of beauty.

Too often in the past, we have thought of the artist as an idler and dilettante and of the lover of arts as somehow sissy or effete. We have done both an injustice. The life of the artist is, in relation to his work, stern and lonely. He has labored hard, often amid deprivation, to perfect his skill. He has turned aside from quick success in order to strip his vision of everything secondary or cheapening. His working life is marked by intense application and intense discipline. As for the lover of arts, it is he who, by subjecting himself to the sometimes disturbing experience of art, sustains the artist—and seeks only the reward that his life will, in consequence, be the more fully lived.

The life of the arts, far from being an interruption, a distraction, in the life of a nation, is very close to the center of a nation's purpose—and is a test of the quality of a nation's civilization.

"The Arts in America"
Creative America
1963

We must never forget that art is not a form of propaganda; it is a form of truth.

In serving his vision of the truth, the artist best serves his nation.

If art is to nourish the roots of our culture, society must set the artist free to follow his vision wherever it takes him.

If sometimes our great artists have been the most critical of our society, it is because their sensitivity and their concern for justice, which must motivate any true artist, make them aware that our nation falls short of its highest potential.

Amherst College
Amherst, Massachusetts
October 26, 1963

Books

Books and libraries and the will to use them are among the most important tools our nation has to diffuse knowledge and to develop our powers of creative wisdom.

National Library Week
April 16, 1961

Canada

We share common values from the past, a common defense line at present, and common aspirations for the future—our future and, indeed, the future of mankind.

Geography has made us neighbors. History has made us friends. Economics has made us partners. And necessity has made us allies. Those whom nature hath so joined together, let no man put asunder.

Address to the Canadian Parliament
Ottawa, Canada
May 17, 1961

Catholicism

You have been taught that each individual has an immortal soul, composed of an intellect which can know truth and a will which is free. Because of this, every Catholic must believe in the essential dignity of the human personality on which any democracy must rest. Believing this, Catholics can never adhere to any political theory which holds that the state is a separate, distinct organization to which allegiance must be paid, rather than a representative institution which derives its powers from the consent of the governed.

In addition, a Catholic's dual allegiance to the Kingdom of God on the one hand prohibits unquestioning obedience on the other to the state as an organic unity.

University of Notre Dame
January, 1950

Never in my public life have I been approached by a representative of the Catholic Church or, for that matter, any other church, to perform an official act which was not consistent with the public interest as I saw it.

Letter, 1957
Quoted in *John Kennedy—
A Political Profile*
by James MacGregor Burns

I am flatly opposed to appointment of an ambassador to the Vatican. . . . Whatever advantages it might have in Rome—and I'm not convinced of these—they would be more than offset by the divisive effect at home.

Washington, D.C.
1958

I am not sure that I would vote for the "Catholic" candidate for President—I hope I am not running as the "Catholic" candidate.

Washington, D.C.
1960

They ask whether I really mean that my oath of office comes above my conscience. . . . There's no conflict. It's part of your conscience to meet your oath.

Washington, D.C.
1960

Are we going to admit to the world that a Jew can be elected Mayor of Dublin, a Protestant can be chosen Foreign Minister in France, a Moslem can serve in the Israeli Parliament—but a Catholic cannot be elected President of the United States?

Society of American Newspapermen

Change

One cannot stand still. As others change, so must we, if we wish to maintain our relative political or economic position.

Wesleyan University
Middletown, Connecticut
October 13, 1959

CHANGE

Let it be clear that this Administration recognizes the value of dissent and daring, that we greet healthy controversy as the hallmark of healthy change.

State of the Union Message
January 29, 1961

We are not lulled by the momentary calm of the sea or the somewhat clearer skies above. We know the turbulence that lies below, and the storms that are beyond the horizon this year. But now the winds of change appear to be blowing more strongly than ever, in the world of Communism as well as our own. For 175 years we have sailed with those winds at our back, and with the tides of human freedom in our favor. We steer our ship with hope, as Thomas Jefferson said, "leaving fear astern."

Today we still welcome those winds of change, and we have every reason to believe that our tide is running strong.

State of the Union Message
January 14, 1963

A great change is at hand, and our task, our obligation, is to make that revolution, that change, peaceful and constructive for all.

Television Address
June 11, 1963

Children

Children are the world's most valuable resource and its best hope for the future. It is a real tragedy that in an era of vast technological progress and scientific achievement millions of children should still suffer from lack of medical care, proper nutrition, adequate education, and be subjected to the handicaps and uncertainties of a low-income, substandard environment.

Washington, D.C.
July 25, 1963

Our children and our grandchildren . . . have no lobby here in Washington.

Our children and grandchildren are not merely statistics toward which we can be indifferent.

Television Address
July 26, 1963

Education is the key to the growth of this country. We must educate our children as our most valuable resource.

AFL-CIO Convention
New York City
November 15, 1963

Church and State

Whatever one's religion in his private life may be, for the officeholder nothing takes precedence over his oath to uphold the Constitution and all its parts—including the First Amendment and the strict separation of church and state.

Separation of church and state is fundamental to our American concept and heritage, and should remain so.

Washington, D.C.
1958

Both church and state should be free to operate, without interference from each other, in their respective areas of jurisdiction. We live in a liberal, democratic society which embraces wide varieties of belief and disbelief. There is no doubt . . . that the pluralism which has developed under our Constitution, providing as it does a framework within which diverse opinions can exist side by side and by their interaction enrich the whole, is the most ideal system yet devised by man.

Letter, 1959
Quoted in John Kennedy—
A Political Profile,
by James MacGregor Burns

In accordance with the clear prohibition of the Constitution, no elementary or secondary school funds are allocated for constructing church schools, or paying church school teachers' salaries; and thus non-public-school children are rightfully not counted in determining the funds each state will receive for its public funds.

Message to Congress
February 20, 1961

Cities

A nation with ugly, crime-infested cities and haphazard suburbs does not present the same image to the world as a nation characterized by bright and orderly development.

Message to Congress
March 9, 1961

A strong America depends on its cities—America's glory and sometimes America's shame.

State of the Union Message
January 11, 1962

We will neglect our cities to our peril, for in neglecting them we neglect the nation.

Message to Congress
January 30, 1962

[31]

Clearsightedness

If the American people more fully comprehend the terrible pressures which discourage acts of political courage . . . they might be less critical of those who take the easier road—and more appreciative of those still able to follow the path of courage.

Profiles in Courage
(Young Readers Edition)

We have comfortably assumed that Marxist dogma and totalitarian repression would produce only stultified minds and ridiculous theories . . . but tonight we are not laughing at the Sputniks.

Loyola College Alumni Banquet
Baltimore, Maryland
February 18, 1958

I am not so much concerned with the right of everyone to say anything he pleases as I am about our need as a self-governing people to hear everything relevant.

National Civil Liberties Conference
Washington, D.C.
April 16, 1959

To state the facts frankly is not to despair for the future nor indict the past.

State of the Union Message
January 29, 1961

The great enemy of the truth is very often not the lie—deliberate, contrived, and dishonest—but the myth—persistent, persuasive and unrealistic.

Yale University
New Haven, Connecticut
June 11, 1962

We must face the fact that the United States is neither omnipotent nor omniscient—that we are only six per cent of the world's population—that we cannot impose our will upon the other 94 per cent of mankind —that we cannot right every wrong or reverse each adversity—and that therefore there cannot be an American solution to every world problem.

University of Washington
Seattle, Washington
November 16, 1961

Commitment

Every generation of Americans has faced a different set of problems in carrying forward . . . [the] abiding purposes of our society. . . . The problems have changed, the purposes have remained constant.

Washington, D.C.
January 1, 1960

We shall be remembered either as the generation that turned this planet into a flaming funeral pyre or the generation that met its vow "to save succeeding generations from the scourge of war."

Address to the United Nations
September 25, 1961

Let the word go forth from this time and place, to friend and foe alike, that the torch has been passed to a new generation of Americans—born in this century, tempered by war, disciplined by a hard and bitter peace, proud of our ancient heritage—and unwilling to witness or permit the slow undoing of those human rights to which this nation has always been committed, and to which we are committed today at home and around the world.

Inaugural Address
January 20, 1961

If we are to go only halfway, or reduce our sights in the face of difficulty . . . it would be better not to go at all.

Message to Congress
May 25, 1961

Peace does not rest in the charters and covenants alone. It lies in the hearts and minds of all people. And in this world . . . no act, no pact, no treaty, no organization can hope to preserve it without the support and the wholehearted commitment of all people.

So let us not rest our hopes on parchment and on paper; let us strive to build peace.

United Nations
September 20, 1963

Community

The people who have come to this country have made America, in the words of one perceptive writer, "a heterogeneous race but a homogeneous nation."

The name "America" was given to this continent by a *German* mapmaker, Martin Waldseemuller, to honor an *Italian* explorer, Amerigo Vespucci. The three ships which discovered America sailed under a *Spanish* flag, were commanded by an *Italian* sea captain, and included in their crews an *Englishman,* an *Irishman,* a *Jew* and a *Negro.*

A Nation of Immigrants

Brotherhood, tolerance, enlightened relations between members of different ethnic groups—these are, after all, simply an extension of the concept upon which all free organized society is based. Some call this concept comity. Some find it in the Golden Rule, others in Rousseau's "social contract." Our Declaration of Independence calls it "the consent of the gov-

[35]

erned." The ancient Romans called it "civitatis filia," or civic friendship.

National Conference of Christians and Jews
Cleveland, Ohio
February 4, 1957

The direction of our destiny is toward community and confidence.

Address to the Conference on
Trade Policy
Washington, D.C.
May 17, 1962

We seek not the world-wide victory of one nation or system, but a world-wide victory of men.

State of the Union Message
January 14, 1963

So let us not be blind to our differences, but let us also direct attention to our common interests and to the means by which those differences can be resolved. And if we cannot end now our differences, at least we can help make the world safe for diversity. For, in the final analysis, our most basic common link is that we all inhabit this planet. We all breathe the same air. We all cherish our children's future. And we are all mortal.

The American University
Washington, D.C.
June 10, 1963

Together we have been partners in adversity; let us also be partners in prosperity.

Frankfurt, West Germany
June 25, 1963

We welcome a stronger partner, for today no nation can build its destiny alone.

Naples, Italy
July 2, 1963

Nothing could more greatly damage our cause than if we and our allies were to believe that peace has already been achieved and that our strength and unity were no longer required.

Television Address
July 26, 1963

Just as the Family of Man is not limited to a single race or religion, neither can it be limited to a single city or country. The Family of Man is more than three billion strong. It lives in more than one hundred nations. Most of its members are not white. Most of them are not Christians. Most of them know nothing about free enterprise or due process of law or the Australian ballot.

Protestant Council of New York City
New York City
November 8, 1963

Complacency

It is right and proper to support vigorously our way of living as being the greatest in the world, but it is not right and proper to be blind to its weaknesses.

Why England Slept

When we should have been decisive we . . . were in doubt. When we should have sailed hard into the wind, we . . . drifted. When we should have planned anew, sacrificed, and marched ahead, we . . . stood still, sought the easy way, and looked to the past.

Democratic Party Convention
Milwaukee, Wisconsin
November 13, 1959

The complacent, the self-indulgent, the soft societies, are about to be swept away with the debris of history.

American Society of Newspaper Editors
Washington, D.C.
April 20, 1961

Complacency or self-congratulation can imperil our security as much as the weapons of our adversaries.

State of the Union Message
January 14, 1963

Conformity

Conformity is the jailer of freedom and the enemy of growth.

United Nations
September 25, 1961

Courage

In the days ahead, only the very courageous will be able to take the hard and unpopular decisions necessary for our survival in the struggle with a powerful enemy.

Washington, D.C.
1956

We want . . . not the sneers of the cynics nor the despair of the fainthearted. We ask . . . enlightenment, vision, illumination.

University of Wisconsin
Madison, Wisconsin
June 16, 1958

It takes great courage to do what you think is right even though it may mean the end of your career and the dislike and criticism of your friends and neighbors.

[39]

In whatever arena of life one may meet the challenge of courage . . . each man must decide for himself the course he will follow. The stories of past courage can define that ingredient—they can teach, they can offer hope, they can provide inspiration. But they cannot supply courage itself. For this each man must look into his own soul.

A nation which has forgotten the quality of courage . . . is not as likely to insist upon or reward that quality in its chosen leaders today . . .

Compromise need not mean cowardice. Indeed, it is frequently the compromisers and conciliators who are faced with the severest tests of political courage . . .

Great crises produce great men and great deeds of courage.

Without belittling the courage with which men have died, we should not forget those acts of courage with which men . . . have *lived*.

Only the very courageous will be able to keep alive the spirit of individualism and dissent which gave birth to this nation, nourished it as an infant and carried it through its severest tests upon the attainment of its maturity.

Profiles in Courage
(Young Readers Edition)

Now, as never before, hundreds of millions of men and women—who had formerly believed that stoic resignation in the face of hunger and disease and darkness was the best one could do—have come alive with a new sense that the means are at hand with which to make for themselves a better life.

If the title deeds of history applied, it is we, the American people, who should be marching at the head of this world-wide revolution, counseling it, helping it come to a healthy fruition.

Washington, D.C.
January 1, 1960

There are many kinds of courage—bravery under fire, courage to risk reputation and friendship and career for convictions which are deeply held. Perhaps the rarest courage of all—for the skill to pursue it is given to very few men—is the courage to wage a silent battle to illuminate the nature of man and the world in which he lives. . . .

"Robert Frost: American Poet"
CBS Television Network
February 26, 1961

Any dangerous spot is tenable if men—brave men —will make it so.

Television Address
July 25, 1961

Deeds

We look for deeds, not words. And we, too, must offer deeds, not words.

University of Rochester
Rochester, New York
October 1, 1959

I do not want it said of our generation what T. S. Eliot wrote in his poem, "The Rock"—"and the wind shall say 'these were decent people, their only monument the asphalt road and a thousand lost golf balls.' " We can do better than that.

Columbus, Ohio
October 17, 1960

With a good conscience our only sure reward, with history the final judge of our deeds, let us go forth to lead the land we love, asking His blessing and His help, but knowing that here on earth God's work must truly be our own. . . . And so, my fellow Americans, ask not what your country can do for you—ask what you can do for your country.

Inaugural Address
January 20, 1961

Last year [1961] we improved the diet of needy people, provided more hot lunches and fresh milk to school children, built more college dormitories, and, for the elderly, expanded private housing, nursing homes, health services and Social Security. But we have just begun.

State of the Union Message
January 11, 1962

Lofty words cannot construct an alliance or maintain it; only concrete deeds can do that.

Frankfurt, West Germany
June 25, 1963

The harsh facts of poverty and social justice will not yield merely to promises and good will.

Inter-American Press Association
Miami Beach, Florida
November 18, 1963

Defense

[Civil Defense] is insurance we trust will never be needed, but insurance which we could never forgive ourselves for foregoing in the event of catastrophe.

Message to Congress
May 25, 1961

Diplomacy and defense are not substitutes for one another. Either alone would fail.

University of Washington
Seattle, Washington
1961

Democracy

The representatives of a democracy cannot run contrary to the basic wishes of the people in any game of bluff.

Democracy is the superior form of government, because it is based on a respect for man as a reasonable being. *For the long run,* then, democracy is superior. But for the short run, democracy has great weaknesses. When it competes with a system of government which cares nothing for permanency, a system built primarily for war, democracy, which is built primarily for peace, is at a disadvantage. And democracy must recognize its weaknesses; it must learn to safeguard its institutions if it hopes to survive.

Democracy and capitalism are institutions which are geared for a world at peace. It is our problem to find a method of protecting them in a world at war.

Democracy is essentially peace-loving; the people don't want to go to war. When they do go, it is with a very firm conviction, because they must believe deeply and strongly in their cause before they consent. This gives them an advantage over a totalitarian system, where the people may find themselves in a war in which they only half believe.

As believers in a democratic system, we have always had faith in its innate powers of resistance. We believe that it will be able to adapt itself to circumstances and, because it is a system based on a respect for the rights of the individual, in the long run it will prove superior. We concede that a dictatorship does have great advantages. We concede that the regimentation and the unification achieved by force and propaganda will give a dictator an initial jump on his opponents. However, we believe that a democracy can, by voluntary action, equal this effort when the emergency comes, and sustain it over a longer period of time.

Why England Slept

The true democracy, living and growing and inspiring, puts its faith in the people—faith that the people will not simply elect men who will represent their views ably and faithfully, but also elect men who will exercise their conscientious judgment—faith that the people will not condemn those whose devotion to principle leads them to unpopular courses, but will reward courage, respect honor and ultimately recognize right.

Profiles in Courage
(Young Readers Edition)

Our . . . task is to demonstrate to the entire world that man's unsatisfied aspiration for economic progress and social justice can best be achieved by free

[45]

men working within a framework of democratic institutions.

> Reception for Latin-American Diplomats
> Washington, D.C.
> March 13, 1961

The state is the servant of the citizen, and not his master.

> State of the Union Message
> January 11, 1962

Democratic government demands that those in opposition accept the defects of today and work toward remedying them within the machinery of peaceful change.

> Inter-American Press Association
> Miami Beach, Florida
> November 18, 1963

Determination

We are reluctant to take risks in this dangerous age; we are reluctant to make hard and unpopular decisions in this popular democracy. But the complex problems . . . will never be solved with an excess of caution or an avoidance of risk.

> Washington, D.C.
> August 21, 1957

We cannot escape our dangers—neither must we let them drive us into panic or narrow isolation. In many areas of the world where the balance of power already rests with our adversaries, the forces of freedom are sharply divided. It is one of the ironies of our time that the techniques of a harsh and repressive system should be able to instill discipline and order in its servants—while the blessings of liberty have too often stood for privilege, materialism, and a life of ease.

But I have a different view of liberty.

Life in 1961 will not be easy. Wishing it, predicting it, even asking for it, will not make it so. There will be further setbacks before the tide is turned. But turn it must. The hopes of all mankind rest upon us.

State of the Union Message
January 30, 1961

Prepare your mind and heart for the task ahead, call forth your strength, and let each devote his energies to the betterment of all . . .

Reception for Latin-American Diplomats
Washington, D.C.
March 13, 1961

Let the record show that our restraint is not inexhaustible.

American Society of Newspaper Editors
Washington, D.C.
April 20, 1961

[47]

This nation was born of revolution and raised in freedom. And we do not intend to leave an open road for despotism.

Our patience at the bargaining table is nearly inexhaustible, though our credulity is limited . . . our hopes for peace are unfailing, while our determination to protect our security is resolute.

Message to Congress
May 25, 1961

If we . . . act out of strength and unity of purpose, with calm determination and steady nerves, using restraint in our words as well as our weapons . . . both peace and freedom will be sustained.

Television Address
July 25, 1961

Terror is not a new weapon. Throughout history it has been used by those who could not prevail either by persuasion or by example. But inevitably they fail, either because men are not afraid to die for a life worth living or because the terrorists themselves come to realize that free men cannot be frightened by threats, and that aggression will meet its own response.

We shall neither commit nor provoke aggression . . . we shall neither flee nor invoke the threat of force

[48]

. . . we shall never negotiate out of fear, and we shall never fear to negotiate.

> United Nations
> September 25, 1961

If . . . [the] history of our progress teaches us anything, it is that man, in his quest for knowledge and progress, is determined and cannot be deterred.

> Rice University
> Houston, Texas
> September 12, 1962

Our problems are man-made, therefore they can be solved by man. And man can be as big as he wants. No problem of human destiny is beyond human beings.

> The American University
> Washington, D.C.
> June 10, 1963

Too often a project is undertaken in the excitement of a crisis, and then it begins to lose its appeal as the problems drag on and the bills pile up. But we must have the steadfastness to see every enterprise through.

> United Nations
> September 20, 1963

[49]

Let us resolve to be the masters, not the victims, of our history, controlling our own destiny without giving way to blind suspicion and emotion . . .

University of Maine
Orono, Maine
October 19, 1963

Where our strength and determination are clear, our words need merely to convey conviction, not belligerence. If we are strong, our character will speak for itself. If we are weak, words will be of no help.

Undelivered speech
Dallas, Texas
Released November 22, 1963

Disarmament

Men no longer pretend that the quest for disarmament is a sign of weakness, for in a spiraling arms race, a nation's security may well be shrinking even as its arms increase.

The weapons of war must be abolished before they abolish us.

To destroy arms . . . is not enough. We must create, even as we destroy, creating world-wide law and

law enforcement as we outlaw world-wide war and
weapons.

United Nations
September 25, 1961

In the long run, it is the constructive possibilities
of that [disarmament] conference, and not the testing of new destructive weapons, on which rest the
hopes of all mankind. However dim those hopes may
sometimes seem, they can never be abandoned.

Television Address
March 2, 1962

The Economy

A political convalescence has no durability unless it
is invigorated by economic therapy.

Washington, D.C.
August 21, 1957

A genuine program of economic development is a
seamless web which cannot be pulled apart or rewoven
from cheaper materials.

Washington, D.C.
March 25, 1958

Modern American capitalism, with its unique combination of public effort and private competitive

enterprise, is dynamic, progressive, and still evolving.

University of Rochester
Rochester, New York
October 1, 1959

Economic progress at home is still the first requirement for economic strength abroad.

Message to Congress
February 6, 1961

It is my determined purpose to be a prudent
steward of the public funds, to obtain a dollar's worth
of results for every dollar we spend. . . .

Message to Congress
March 24, 1961

A chaotic patchwork of inconsistent and often
obsolete legislation and regulation . . . does not fully
reflect either the dramatic changes in technology of
the past half-century or the parallel changes in the
structure of competition.

Message to Congress
April 4, 1962

We want prosperity, and in a free enterprise system there can be no prosperity without profit. We
want a growing economy, and there can be no growth
without the investment that is inspired and financed
by profit.

United States Chamber of Commerce
April 30, 1962

[52]

The mere absence of recession is not growth.

> State of the Union Message
> January 14, 1963

A balanced and stable economy is essential if we are to meet both domestic and world challenges in the coming years . . .

> Message to Congress
> January 31, 1963

Education

Having experienced for themselves the handicaps of illiteracy, they [the immigrants] were determined that their children would have the advantages of education.

> *A Nation of Immigrants*

The goal of education is the advancement of knowledge and the dissemination of truth . . .

> Harvard University
> Cambridge, Massachusetts
> 1956

We cannot continue to pay our college faculties and school teachers less for improving the minds of our children than we pay plumbers and steamfitters for improving our homes.

Loyola College Alumni Banquet
Baltimore, Maryland
February 19, 1958

The human mind is our fundamental resource.

Message to Congress
February 20, 1961

It is no exaggeration to say that the struggle in which we are now engaged may well be won or lost in the classrooms of America.

Social Science Foundation
Denver University
Denver, Colorado
February 24, 1958

Arms and science alone will not save us. In our concern for the future of America we dare not neglect the education of its politicians.

University of Wisconsin
Madison, Wisconsin
June 16, 1958

It was in our schools that some of the most renowned African leaders learned about the dignity and equality of men, and saw in practice the virtues of representative government, widespread education, and economic opportunity.

Washington University
Lincoln, Nebraska
October 13, 1959

Our twin goals must be: a new standard of excellence in education, and the availability of such excellence to all who are willing and able to pursue it.

Our progress as a nation can be no swifter than our progress in education.

Message to Congress
February 20, 1961

Our ultimate goal must be a basic education for all who wish to learn.

Reception for Latin-American Diplomats
Washington, D.C.
March 13, 1961

Schools are supported by our people because our people realize that this country has needed in the past, and needs today as never before, educated men and women who are committed to the cause of freedom.

University of Washington
Seattle, Washington
November 16, 1961

"Civilization," said H. G. Wells, "is a race between education and catastrophe." It is up to you in this Congress to determine the winner of that race.

State of the Union Message
January 11, 1962

[55]

EDUCATION

Thomas Jefferson once said that if you expect a people to be ignorant and free you expect what never was and never will be.

Washington, D.C.
February 16, 1962

We need to strengthen our nation by investing in our youth. The future of any country which is dependent upon the will and wisdom of its citizens is damaged, and irreparably damaged, whenever any of its children are not educated to the full extent of their talents, from grade school through graduate school.

State of the Union Message
January 14, 1963

I do not say that the federal government should take over responsibility for education; that is neither desirable nor feasible. Instead, its participation should be selective, stimulative and, where possible, transitional . . .

The proper federal role is to identify national education goals and to help local, state, and private authorities build the necessary roads to reach these goals.

Increasing the quality and availability of education is vital to both our national security and our domestic well-being. A free nation can rise no higher than the standard of excellence set in its schools and colleges.

Education cannot easily or wisely be divided into separate parts. Each part is linked to the other.

Message to Congress
January 29, 1963

If our nation is to meet the goal of giving every American child a fair chance—because an uneducated child makes an uneducated parent, who in another day produces another uneducated child—we must move ahead swiftly . . . and recognize that segregation in education . . . brings with it serious handicaps to large proportions of the population.

No country can possibly move ahead, no free society can possibly be sustained, unless it has an educated citizenry whose quality of mind and heart permit it to take part in the complicated and sophisticated decisions that are demanded and pour out not only upon the President and upon the Congress, but upon all of the citizens, who exercise the ultimate power.

San Diego State College
San Diego, California
June 6, 1963

Only an America which has fully educated its citizens is fully capable of tackling the complex problems and perceiving the hidden dangers of the world in which we live.

Undelivered Address
before the Dallas Citizens Council
Released November 22, 1963

Employment

Too many unemployed are still looking for the blessings of prosperity.

State of the Union Message
January 11, 1962

We believe that if men have the talent to invent new machines that put men out of work, they have the talent to put those men back to work.

Wheeling, West Virginia
September 27, 1962

Civil rights legislation is important. But to make that legislation effective, we need jobs in the United States. . . . No one gains from a fair employment practice bill if there is no employment to be had. No one gains by being admitted to a lunch counter if he has no money to spend. No one gains from attending a better school if he doesn't have a job after graduation. No one thinks much of the right to own a good home, or to sleep in a good hotel, or go to the theatre, if he has no work and no money.

State of the Union Message
January 14, 1963

Racial discrimination in employment is especially injurious both to its victims and to the national economy. It results in a great waste of human resources and creates serious community problems. It is, moreover, inconsistent with the democratic principle that no man should be denied employment commensurate with his abilities because of his race or creed or ancestry.

Message to Congress
February 28, 1963

Equality

Equality in America has never meant literal equality of condition or capacity; there will always be inequalities in character and ability in any society. Equality has meant rather that, in the words of the Declaration of Independence, "all men are created equal . . . [and] are endowed by their Creator with certain inalienable rights"; it has meant that in a democratic society there should be no inequalities in opportunities or in freedom.

We have come to realize in modern times that the "melting pot" need not mean the end of particular ethnic identities or traditions.

A Nation of Immigrants

The denial of constitutional rights to some of our fellow Americans on account of race, at the ballot box and elsewhere, disturbs the national conscience and subjects us to the charge of world opinion that our democracy is not equal to the high promise of our heritage.

State of the Union Message
January 29, 1961

Our nation can ill afford to tolerate the growth of an underprivileged and underpaid class.

Letter to the President of the Senate
February 7, 1961

Whenever one taxpayer is permitted to pay less, someone else must be asked to pay more.

Message to Congress
April 20, 1961

America stands for progress in human rights as well as economic affairs, and a strong America requires the assurance of full and equal rights to all its citizens, of any race or of any color.

State of the Union Message
January 11, 1962

This nation was founded by men of many nations and backgrounds. It was founded on the principle that all men are created equal, and that the rights of every man are diminished when the rights of one man are threatened.

It ought to be possible . . . for every American to enjoy the privileges of being American without regard to his race or his color . . .

In short, every American ought to have the right to be treated as he would wish to be treated, as one would wish his children to be treated.

Television Address
June 11, 1963

This nation is now engaged in a continuing debate about the rights of a portion of its citizens. That debate will go on, and those rights will expand, until the standard forged by the nation's founders has been reached—and all Americans enjoy equal opportunity and liberty under law.

Vanderbilt University
Nashville, Tennessee
1963

The United States of America is opposed to discrimination and persecution on grounds of race and religion anywhere in the world, *including our own nation*. We are working to right the wrongs of our own country.

United Nations
September 20, 1963

Faith

We must recognize that human collaboration is not enough, that in times such as these we must reach beyond ourselves if we are to seek ultimate courage and infinite wisdom.

The guiding principle and prayer of this nation has been, is now, and shall ever be, "In God We Trust."

Dedication Breakfast of the
International Christian Leadership
February 9, 1961

I believe the problems of human destiny are not beyond the reach of human beings.

United Nations
September 20, 1963

There can be no progress if people have no faith in tomorrow.

Inter-American Press Association
Miami Beach, Florida
November 18, 1963

Farming

The farmer does not want to ration poverty—he wants to share abundance.

Midwest Farm Conference
Springfield, Illinois
October 24, 1959

It is deeply in the interest of all Americans that our agriculture be not only progressive but prosperous.

Farming remains our largest industry. . . . It employs . . . more people than steel, automobiles, public utilities and the transportation industry combined.

Message to Congress
March 16, 1961

Foreign Aid

We must narrow the gap between abundance here at home and near-starvation abroad.

Memorandum to federal agencies
on duties of Director of Food for Peace Program
January 24, 1961

In a presently troubled world we cannot be a peace-maker if we are not also the protector of those individuals as well as nations who cast with us their personal liberty and hopes for the future.

Letter to Abraham Ribicoff
January 27, 1961

We have a positive interest in helping less developed nations provide decent living standards for their people and achieve sufficient strength, self-respect, and independence to become self-reliant members of the community of nations.

Its [foreign aid program] fundamental task is to help make an historical demonstration that in the twentieth century as in the nineteenth, in the southern half of the globe as in the north, economic growth and political democracy can develop hand in hand.

A program of assistance to the underprivileged nations must continue because the nation's interest and the cause of political freedom require it.

Message to Congress
March 22, 1961

These programs [Peace Corps, Food for Peace Program, Alliance for Progress] help people; and, by helping people, they help freedom.

The processes of growth are gradual, bearing fruit in a decade, not a day. Our successes will be neither quick nor dramatic. But if these programs [Mutual Assistance Program, etc.] were ever to be ended, our failures in a dozen countries would be sudden and would be certain.

State of the Union Message
January 14, 1963

Freedom

Freedom and security are but opposite sides of the same coin—and the free expression of ideas is not more expendable, but far more essential, in a period of challenge and crisis.

Without freedom of speech, freedom of assembly, freedom of religion, freedom of the press, equal protection of the laws, and other inalienable rights, men could not govern themselves intelligently.

National Civil Liberties Conference
Washington, D.C.
April 16, 1959

No people can become strong in a climate of servitude and social indignity.

Conference of The American Society
of African Culture
New York City
June 28, 1959

[65]

My fellow citizens of the world: ask not what America will do for you, but what together we can do for the freedom of man.

In the long history of the world, only a few generations have been granted the role of defending freedom in its hours of maximum danger. I do not shrink from this responsibility—I welcome it. I do not believe that any of us would exchange places with any other people or any other generation. The energy, the faith, the devotion which we bring to this endeavor will light our country and all who serve it—and the glow from that fire can truly light the world.

Inaugural Address
January 20, 1961

All our early revolutionary leaders, I think, echoed the words of Thomas Jefferson that "the disease of liberty is catching." And some of you may remember the exchange between Benjamin Franklin and Thomas Paine. Benjamin Franklin said, "Where freedom lives, there is my home." And Thomas Paine said, "Where freedom is not, there is my home." I think all of us who believe in freedom feel a sense of community with all those who are free, but I think we also feel an even stronger sense of community with those who are not free but who someday will be free.

African Freedom Day Reception
Washington, D.C.
April 15, 1961

If the self-discipline of the free cannot match the iron discipline of the mailed fist, in economic, political, scientific, and all the other kinds of struggles, as well as the military, then the peril to freedom will continue to rise.

American Society of Newspaper Editors
Washington, D.C.
April 20, 1961

We stand for freedom. That is our conviction for ourselves; that is our only commitment to others.

We are not against any man, or any nation, or any system, except as it is hostile to freedom.

Message to Congress
May 25, 1961

A "peace treaty" which would destroy the peace would be a fraud. A "free city" which was not genuinely free would suffocate freedom and would be an infamy.

United Nations
September 25, 1961

We must be patient. We must be determined. We must be courageous. We must accept both risks and burdens. But with the will and the work, freedom will prevail.

Television Report
June 6, 1961

FREEDOM

It is the fate of this generation—of you in the Congress and of me as President—to live with a struggle we did not start, in a world we did not make. But the pressures of life are not always distributed by choice. And while no nation has ever faced such a challenge, no nation has ever been so ready to seize the burden and the glory of freedom.

And in this high endeavor, may God watch over the United States of America.

State of the Union Message
January 11, 1962

Entrusted with the fate and future of our states and nation, [we] declare now our vow to do our part to lift the weights from the shoulders of all, to join other men and nations in preserving both peace and freedom, and to regard any threat to the peace or freedom of one as a threat to the peace and freedom of all.

Independence Hall
Philadelphia, Pennsylvania
July 4, 1962

The cost of freedom is always high, but Americans have always paid it.

Television Address
October 22, 1962

Wherever nations are willing to help themselves, we stand ready to help them build new bulwarks of freedom.

State of the Union Message
January 14, 1963

[68]

Freedom is more than the rejection of tyranny . . . prosperity is more than an escape from want . . . partnership is more than a sharing of power. These are all, above all, great human adventures. They must have meaning and conviction and purpose . . .

Frankfurt, West Germany
June 25, 1963

Freedom is indivisible, and when one man is enslaved, all are not free.

West Berlin
June 26, 1963

We believe that in all the world . . . people must be free to choose their own future, without discrimination or dictation, without coercion or subversion.

United Nations
September 20, 1963

Truth is stronger than error, and . . . freedom is more enduring than coercion. And in the contest for a better life, all the world can be a winner.

United Nations
September 20, 1963

Together let us build sturdy mansions of freedom, mansions that all the world can admire and copy, but that no tyrant can ever enter.

Rome, Italy
July 1, 1963

The Future

Let us not seek the Republican answer or the Democratic answer, but the right answer. Let us not seek to fix the blame for the past. Let us accept our own responsibility for the future.

Loyola College Alumni Banquet
Baltimore, Maryland
February 18, 1958

I am not fearful of the future. We must be patient. We must be courageous. We must accept both risks and burdens, but with the will and the work freedom will prevail.

Liberty and independence and self-determination, not communism, is the future of man, and . . . free men will have the will and the resources to win the struggle for freedom.

Television Address
June 6, 1961

We love our country, not for what it was, though it has always been great—not for what it is, though of this we are deeply proud—but for what it someday can and, through the efforts of us all, someday will be.

National Industrial Conference Board
Washington, D.C.
February 13, 1961

The way of the past shows clearly that freedom, not coercion, is the wave of the future.

> State of the Union Message
> January 11, 1962

Human resources and natural resources are inexorably intertwined, and tomorrow's children, if they are to manage this land well, will need the precision of scientifically attuned minds, coupled with a sensitivity to their fellow men and creatures.

> November, 1963

The wave of the future is not the conquest of the world by a single dogmatic creed, but the liberation of the diverse energies of free nations and free men.

> University of California
> Berkeley, California
> March 23, 1962

The vast stretches of the unknown and the unanswered and the unfinished still far outstrip our collective comprehension.

> Rice University
> Houston, Texas
> September 12, 1962

Upon our achievement of greater vitality and strength here at home hang our fate and future in the world.

You and I are privileged to serve the great Republic in what could be the most decisive decade in its long history. The choices we make, for good or ill, will affect the welfare of generations yet unborn.

State of the Union Message
January 14, 1963

We are all idealists. We are all visionaries. Let it not be said of this Atlantic generation that we left ideals and visions to the past, nor purpose and determination to our adversaries. We have come too far, we have sacrificed too much, to disdain the future now.

Those who look only to the past are certain to miss the future.

Frankfurt, West Germany
June 25, 1963

Let me ask you . . . to lift your eyes beyond the dangers of today to the hopes of tomorrow . . .

Berlin, Germany
June 26, 1963

I look forward toward a great future for America, a future in which our country will match its military strength with our moral strength, its wealth with our wisdom, its power with our purpose. I look forward to an America which will not be afraid of grace and beauty, which will protect the beauty of our natural environment, which will preserve the great old American houses and squares and parks of our nation's past, and which will build handsome and balanced cities for our future. . . . And I look forward to an America which commands respect throughout the world not only for its strength but for its civilization as well.

November, 1963

Heritage

The Bill of Rights is the guardian of our security as well as our liberty.

Let us not be afraid of debate or dissent—let us encourage it. For if we should ever abandon these basic American traditions in the name of fighting Communism, what would it profit us to win the whole world when we have lost our own soul?

National Civil Liberties Conference
Washington, D.C.
April 16, 1959

Our national conservation effort must include the complete spectrum of resources: air, water, and land; fuels, energy, and minerals; soils, forests, and forage; fish and wildlife. Together they make up the world of nature which surrounds us—a vital part of the American heritage.

Address to Congress
March 1, 1962

It is our task, in our times and our generation, to hand down undiminished to those who come after us, as was handed down to us by those who went before, the natural wealth and beauty which is ours.

Dedication of the
National Wildlife Federation Building
Washington, D.C.
March 3, 1961

When my great-grandfather left here [Ireland] to be a cooper in East Boston, he carried nothing with him except two things; a strong religious faith and a strong desire for liberty. I am glad to say that all of his great-grandchildren have valued that inheritance.

New Ross, Ireland
June 27, 1963

Hope

We should not let our fears hold us back from pursuing our hopes.

Washington, D.C.
December 11, 1959

Unless necessary social reforms, including land and tax reform, are freely made; unless we broaden the opportunity of all our people; unless the great mass of Americans share in increasing prosperity, then our alliance, our revolution, our dream, and our freedom will fail.

> Reception for Latin-American Diplomats
> Washington, D.C.
> March 13, 1961

Self-determination is but a slogan if the future holds no hope.

> United Nations
> September 25, 1961

Our overriding obligation . . . is to fulfill the world's hopes by fulfilling our own.

> State of the Union Message
> January 11, 1962

Hope must be tempered with caution.

> State of the Union Message
> January 14, 1963

Today the fear is a little less and the hopes a little greater.

> Washington, D.C.
> October 7, 1963

That hope [for the future] is for a hemisphere where every man has enough to eat and a chance to work, where every child can learn and every family can find decent shelter. It is for a hemisphere where every man, from the American Negro to the Indian of the Altiplano, can be liberated from the bonds of social injustice, free to pursue his own talents as far as they will take him, allowed to participate in the fruits of progress.

Inter-American Press Association
Miami Beach, Florida
November 18, 1963

For two thousand years, every generation, or most generations, have been faced with the most terrible problems ever seen. They all have been solved by humans with God's help. If they could do it, why can't we?

Comment to his father,
quoted by Hugh Sidey,
in *John F. Kennedy, President*

Ideas

It takes time to change men's minds, and it takes violent shocks to change an entire nation's psychology.

Why England Slept

The duty of the scholar—particularly in a republic such as ours—is to contribute his objective views and his sense of liberty to the affairs of his state and nation.

University of Wisconsin
Madison, Wisconsin
June 16, 1958

What we need now in this nation, more than atomic power, or airpower, or financial, industrial, or even manpower, is brain power.

What we need most of all is a constant flow of new ideas—a government and a nation and a press and a public opinion which respect new ideas and respect the people who have them. Our country has surmounted great crises in the past, not because of our wealth, not because of our rhetoric, not because we had longer cars and whiter iceboxes and bigger television screens than anyone else, but because our ideas were more compelling and more penetrating and wiser and more enduring. And perhaps more important, we encouraged all ideas—the unorthodox as well as the conventional, the radical as well as the traditional.

National Civil Liberties Conference
Washington, D.C.
April 16, 1959

A man may die, nations may rise and fall, but an idea lives on. Ideas have endurance without death.

Greenville, North Carolina
February 8, 1963

The problems of the world cannot possibly be solved by skeptics or cynics whose horizons are limited by the obvious realities. We need men who can dream of things that never were . . .

Dublin, Ireland
June 28, 1963

Immigration

The continuous immigration of the nineteenth and early twentieth centuries . . . reminded every American, old and new, that change is the essence of life, and that American society is a process, not a conclusion.

Oscar Handlin has said, "Once I thought to write a history of immigrants in America. Then I discovered that the immigrants *were* American history." In the same sense, we cannot really speak of a particular "immigrant contribution" to America because all Americans have been immigrants or the descendants of immigrants.

Immigration is by definition a gesture of faith in social mobility. It is the expression in action of a positive belief in the possibility of a better life.

Every American who ever lived, with the exception of one group, was either an immigrant himself or a descendant of immigrants. The exception? Will Rogers, part Cherokee Indian, said that his ancestors were at the dock to meet the Mayflower.

Our investment in new citizens has always been a valuable source of our strength.

The contribution of immigrants can be seen in every aspect of our national life. We see it in religion, in politics, in business, in the arts, in education, even in athletics and in entertainment. There is no part of our nation that has not been touched by our immigrant background.

Yesterday's immigrants . . . have supplied a continuous flow of creative abilities and ideas that have enriched our nation.

The immigrants we welcome today and tomorrow will carry on this tradition and help us to retain, reinvigorate and strengthen the American spirit.

Each world crisis is met by a new exception to the Immigration and Nationality Act of 1952. Each exception reflects the natural humanitarian impulses of the American people, which is in keeping with our traditions of shelter to the homeless and refuge for the oppressed.

The same things are said today of Puerto Ricans and Mexicans that were once said of Irish, Italians, Germans and Jews: "They'll never adjust; they can't learn the language; they won't be absorbed."

More than 42 million immigrants have come to our shores since the beginning of our history as a nation. Why they came here and what they did after they arrived make up the story of America. They came for a variety of reasons from every quarter of the world, representing almost every race, almost every religion and almost every creed. Through their ingenuity, their industry and their imagination, they were able to create out of a wilderness a thriving and prosperous nation—and, through their dedication to liberty and freedom, they helped to build a government reflecting man's most cherished ideals.

A Nation of Immigrants

Independence

The most powerful single force in the world today is neither Communism nor capitalism, neither the H-bomb nor the guided missile—it is man's eternal desire to be free and independent.

Washington, D.C.
July 2, 1957

As a nation, we think not of war but of peace; not of crusades of conflict but of covenants of cooperation; not of the pageantry of imperialism but of the pride of new states freshly risen to independence.

Washington, D.C.
February 19, 1958

The theory of independence, as old as man himself, was not invented in this hall [Independence Hall, Philadelphia], but it was in this hall that the theory became a practice, that the word went out to all the world that "the God who gave us life gave us liberty at the same time."

And today this nation, conceived in revolution, nurtured in liberty, matured in independence, has no intention of abdicating its leadership in that world-wide movement for independence to any nation or society committed to systematic human suppression.

To read ... [the Declaration of Independence] today is to hear a trumpet call. For that Declaration unleashed not merely a revolution against the British, but a revolution in human affairs.

> Independence Hall
> Philadelphia, Pennsylvania
> July 4, 1962

Integrity

Civility is not a sign of weakness, and sincerity is always subject to proof.

> Inaugural Address
> January 20, 1961

We do not intend to be lectured on "intervention" by those whose character was stamped for all time on the bloody streets of Budapest.

American Society of Newspaper Editors
Washington, D.C.
April 20, 1961

The basis of effective confidence is endangered when ethical standards falter or appear to falter.

No responsibility of government is more fundamental than the responsibility of maintaining the highest standards of ethical behavior by those who conduct the public business.

Inevitably, the moral standards of a society influence the conduct of all who live within it, the governed and those who govern.

No web of statute or regulation, however intricately conceived, can hope to deal with the myriad possible challenges to a man's integrity or his devotion to the public interest.

There can be no dissent from the principle that all officials must act with unwavering integrity, absolute impartiality and complete devotion to the public interest.

Message to Congress
April 27, 1961

Dissent does not mean disunity, and disagreement can surely be healthy, so long as we avoid . . . any ill-tempered or ill-conceived remarks which may encourage those who hope to divide and conquer.

Address to the Conference on Trade Policy
Washington, D.C.
May 17, 1962

We cannot negotiate with those who say, "What's mine is mine and what's yours is negotiable."

Television Address
July 25, 1961

A nation can be no stronger abroad than she is at home. Only an America which practices what it preaches about equal rights and social justice will be respected by those whose choice affects our future.

Undelivered address
Dallas, Texas
Released November 22, 1963

The Irish

The Irish were the first to endure the scorn and discrimination later to be inflicted, to some degree at least, on each successive wave of immigrants by already settled "Americans." In speech and dress they seemed foreign; they were poor and unskilled; and they were arriving in overwhelming numbers. The Irish are perhaps the only people in our history with the distinction of having a political party, the Know-Nothings, formed against them. Their religion was later also the target of the American Protective Association and, in this country, the Ku Klux Klan.

A Nation of Immigrants

I want to express my pleasure at being back from whence I came. There is an impression in Washington that there are no Kennedys left in Ireland, that they are all in Washington, so I wonder if there are any Kennedys in this audience. Could you hold up your hand so I can see?

Well, I. am glad to see a few cousins who didn't catch the boat.

It seems to me that in these dangerous days when the struggle for freedom is world-wide against an armed doctrine, that Ireland and its experience has one special significance, and that is that the people's fight, which John Boyle O'Reilly said outlived a thousand years, that it was possible for a people over hundreds of years of foreign domination and religious persecution—it was possible for that people to maintain their national identity and their strong faith. And therefore those who may feel that in these difficult times, who may believe that freedom may be on the run, or that some nations may be permanently sub-

[84]

jugated and eventually wiped out, would do well to remember Ireland.

Wexford, Ireland
June 27, 1963

I don't want to give the impression that every member of this Administration in Washington is Irish—it just seems that way.

It is important that those of us who happen to be of Irish descent who come to Ireland recognize an even stronger bond which exists between Ireland and the United States, between Europe and the United States, between Latin America and the United States, between the people of Africa, the people of Asia, between all people who wish to be free. This is the most important association, the most important kinship. And I come to this island which has been identified with that effort for a thousand years, which was the first country in the twentieth century to lead what is the most powerful tide of the twentieth century—the desire for national independence, the desire to be free. And I come here in 1963 and find that strong tide still beats, still runs. . . .

Cork, Ireland
June 28, 1963

The White House was designed by James Hoban, a noted Irish-American architect, and I have no doubt that he believed by incorporating several features of the Dublin style he would make it more homelike for any President of Irish descent. It was a long wait, but I appreciate his efforts.

Our two nations, divided by distance, have been united by history. No people ever believed more deeply in the cause of Irish freedom than the people of the United States. And no country contributed more to building my own than your sons and daughters. . . .

This is an extraordinary country. George Bernard Shaw, speaking as an Irishman, summed up an approach to life: "Other people," he said, "see things and . . . say: 'Why?' . . . But I dream things that never were—and I say 'Why not?' "

It is that quality of the Irish—that remarkable combination of hope, confidence, and imagination—that is needed more than ever today.

Your future is as promising as your past is proud . . .

Irish Parliament
Dublin, Ireland
June 28, 1963

If the day were clear enough, and if you went down the bay, and you looked west, and your sight was good enough, you would see Boston, Massachusetts. And if you did, you would see down working at the docks

[86]

there some Doughertys and Flahertys and Ryans and cousins of yours who have gone to Boston and made good.

Galway, Ireland
June 29, 1963

Israel

Let us make clear that we will never turn our back on our steadfast friends in Israel, whose adherence to the democratic way must be admired by all friends of freedom.

Eastern Oregon College of Education
La Grande, Oregon
November 9, 1959

The Middle East today is a monument to Western misunderstanding.

Washington, D.C.
1959

Israel is the bright light now shining in the Middle East. We, and ultimately Israel's neighbors, have much to learn from this center of democratic illumination, of unprecedented economic development, of human pioneering and intelligence and perseverance.

Washington, D.C.
1959

[87]

Israel . . . embodying all the characteristics of a Western democracy and having long passed the threshold of economic development, shares with the West a tradition of civil liberties, of cultural freedom, of parliamentary democracy, of social mobility.

The Jewish state found its fulfillment during a time when it bore witness, to use the words of Markham, to humanity betrayed, "plundered, profaned, and disinherited."

As we observe the inspiring experiences of Israel, we know that we must make the effort—and that we can once again demonstrate that "rain follows the plow."

B'nai Zion Banquet
New York City
February 9, 1959

Knowledge

As men conduct the pursuit of knowledge, they create a world which freely unites national diversity and international partnership.

The pursuit of knowledge . . . rests . . . on the idea of a world based on diversity, self-determination, freedom.

University of California
Berkeley, California
March 23, 1963

We meet in an hour of change and challenge, in a decade of hope and fear, in an age of both knowledge and ignorance. The greater our knowledge increases, the greater our ignorance unfolds.

Rice University
Houston, Texas
September 12, 1962

Latin America

I have called on all people of this hemisphere to join in a new Alliance for Progress—*Alianza para Progreso*—a vast cooperative effort, unparalleled in magnitude and nobility of purpose, to satisfy the basic needs of the American people for homes, work, and land, health and schools—*techo, trabajo y tierra, salud y escuela.*

Our Alliance for Progress is an alliance of free governments, and it must work to eliminate tyranny from a hemisphere in which it has no rightful place.

We call for a social change by free men—change in the spirit of Washington and Jefferson, of Bolívar and San Martín and Martín—not change which seeks to impose on men tyrannies which we cast out a century and a half ago. Our motto is what it has always

[89]

been—progress, yes; tyranny, no! *Progreso, si; tiranía, no!*

We propose to complete the revolution of the Americas, to build a hemisphere where all men can hope for a suitable standard of living, and all can live out their lives in dignity and in freedom.

I say to the men and women of the Americas—to the *campesino* in the fields, to the *obrero* in the cities, to the *estudiante* in the schools—prepare your mind and heart for the task ahead—call forth your strength and let each devote his energies to the betterment of all, so that your children and our children in this hemisphere can find an ever richer and freer life.

Reception for Latin American Diplomats
Washington, D.C.
March 13, 1961

Our task is to build a society of men and women conscious of their individual identity, of their national aspirations, and also of their common hemisphere interest.

Council of the Organization of American States
April 14, 1961

While the name, Alliance for Progress, might be new, the ideas . . . are not the monopoly of any single American state . . .

Statement on Adlai Stevenson's
Mission to South America
May 29, 1961

We live in a hemisphere whose own revolution has given birth to the most powerful forces of the modern age—the search for freedom and self-fulfillment of man.

> Inter-American Economic and Social Conference
> August 5, 1961

Law

A community without law is but a shell.

We far prefer world law, in the age of self-determination, to world war, in the age of mass extermination.

> Address to the United Nations
> September 25, 1961

Our nation is founded on the principle that observance of the law is the eternal safeguard of liberty and defiance of the law is the surest road to tyranny. . . . Even among law-abiding men few laws are universally loved, but they are uniformly respected and not resisted.

Americans are free to disagree with the law, but not to disobey it. For in a government of laws and not of men, no man, however prominent and powerful, and no mob, however unruly or boisterous, is entitled to defy a court of law. If this country should ever reach the point where any man or group of men by force or threat of force could long defy the commands of our court and our Constitution, then no law would stand free from doubt, no judge would be sure of his writ, and no citizen would be safe from his neighbors.

Television Address
September 30, 1962

Leadership

Leaders are responsible for their failures only in the governing sector and cannot be held responsible for the failure of a nation as a whole.

Why England Slept

When at some future date the high court of history sits in judgment on each of us . . . our success or failure . . . will be measured by the answers to four questions:

. . . were we truly men of courage? . . .
. . . were we truly men of judgment? . . .
. . . were we truly men of integrity? . . .
. . . were we truly men of dedication? . . .

Massachusetts State Legislature
January 9, 1961

Public officials are not a group apart. They inevitably reflect the moral tone of the society in which they live.

High ethical standards can be maintained only if the leaders of government provide a personal example of dedication to the public service . . .

> Message to Congress
> April 27, 1961

I need your good will, and your support, and, above all, your prayers.

> Report to the People
> July 25, 1961

Members of the Congress, the Constitution makes us not rivals for power but partners for progress. We are all trustees for the American people, custodians of the American heritage.

> State of the Union Message
> January 11, 1962

Liberty

Every ethnic minority, in seeking its own freedom, helped strengthen the fabric of liberty in American life.

> *A Nation of Immigrants*

[93]

The American tradition has demonstrated . . . that freedom is the ally of security . . . and that liberty is the architect of abundance.

> National Civil Liberties Conference
> Washington, D.C.
> April 16, 1959

Let every nation know, whether it wishes us well or ill, that we shall pay any price, bear any burden, meet any hardship, support any friend, oppose any foe, to assure the survival and success of liberty.

> Inaugural Address
> January 20, 1961

Liberty is not easy to find. It is a search that takes us on a hard road.

> Presentation of the Medal of Freedom
> to Paul Henri Spaak, General Secretary, NATO
> February 21, 1961

Leonardo da Vinci was not only an artist and a sculptor, an architect and a scientist . . . [but also] a military engineer, an occupation which he pursued, he tells us, in order to preserve the chief gift of nature, which is liberty.

> The "Mona Lisa" Ceremony
> National Gallery of Art
> Washington, D.C.
> January 8, 1963

Unless liberty flourishes in all lands, it cannot flourish in one. Conceived in one hall, it must be carried out in many.

Our liberty . . . is endangered if we pause for the passing moment, if we rest on our achievements, if we resist the pace of progress.

Frankfurt, Germany
June 25, 1963

The truth does not die. The desire for liberty cannot be fully suppressed.

West Berlin
June 26, 1963

Natural Resources

Wise investment in a resource program today will return vast dividends tomorrow, and failures to act now may be opportunities lost forever.

Message to Congress
February 23, 1961

Our future greatness and our strength depend upon the continued abundant use of our natural resources.

NATURAL RESOURCES

It is our task in our time and in our generation to hand down undiminished to those who come after us, as was handed down to us by those who went before, the natural wealth and beauty which is ours . . .

At the Inauguration, Robert Frost read the poem which began, "The land was ours before we were the land's," meaning, in part, that this new land of ours sustained us before we were a nation. And although we are now the land's, a nation of people matched to a continent, we still draw our strength and sustenance, in this city and in every other city across the country, from the earth.

> Dedication Ceremonies,
> National Wildlife Federation Building
> Washington, D.C.
> March 3, 1961

Americans have been richly endowed with a land that is both beauteous and bountiful. Our greatness today rests in part on this good gift of geography that is the United States; but what is important for tomorrow is what the people of America do with their conservation legacy.

> Convention Center
> Las Vegas, Nevada
> September 28, 1963

Government must provide a national policy framework for this new conservation emphasis; but in the final analysis it must be done by the people them-

selves. The American people are not by nature waste-
ful. They are not unappreciative of our inheritance.
But unless we, as a country, with the support, and
sometimes the direction, of Government, working
with State leaders, working with the community,
working with all of our citizens, we are going to leave
an entirely different inheritance in the next twenty-
five years than the one we found.

Pinchot Institute for Conservation Studies
Milford, Pennsylvania
September 24, 1963

Every time an acre of land disappears into private
development or exploitation, an acre of land which
could be used for the people, we have lost a chance.
We will never get it back.

University of North Dakota
Grand Forks, North Dakota
September 25, 1963

Too many people east of the Mississippi are un-
aware of what golden resources we have in our own
United States.

Dedication of Whiskeytown Dam and Reservoir
Whiskeytown, California
September 28, 1963

The earth can be an abundant mother . . . if we
learn to use her with skill and wisdom, to heal her

[97]

wounds, replenish her vitality and utilize her potentialities. . . .

International scientific cooperation is indispensable if human knowledge of the ocean is to keep pace with human needs.

National Academy of Sciences
Washington, D.C.
October 22, 1963

I look forward to an America which will not be afraid of grace and beauty, which will protect the beauty of our natural environment. . . .

November, 1963

Negroes

Only in the case of the Negro has the melting pot failed to bring a minority into the full stream of American life.

A Nation of Immigrants

If a Negro is born—and this is true also of Puerto Ricans and Mexicans in some of our cities—he has about half as much chance to get through college as a white student. He has about half as much chance to be a professional man, and about half as much chance to own a house. He has about four times as much chance that he'll be out of work in his life as the white baby. I think we can do better.

Television-Radio Debate
Chicago, Illinois
September 26, 1960

We do not want a Negro who could be a doctor, in a city short of doctors, working as a messenger.

East Los Angeles College
November 1, 1960

Despite humiliation and deprivation, the Negro retained his loyalty to the United States and to democratic institutions. He showed his loyalty by brave service in two world wars, by the rejection of extreme or violent policies, by a quiet and proud determination to work for long-denied rights within the framework of the American Constitution.

Emancipation Day Message
Washington, D.C.
September 22, 1962

We preach freedom around the world, and we mean it, and we cherish our freedom here at home; but are we to say to the world and, much more importantly, to each other, that this is a land of the free except for the Negroes; that we have no second-class citizens except Negroes; that we have no class or caste system, no ghettos, no master race except with respect to Negroes?

If an American, because his skin is dark, cannot eat lunch in a restaurant open to the public, if he cannot send his children to the best public school available, if he cannot vote for the public officials who represent him, if, in short, he cannot enjoy the full and free life which all of us want, then who among us would be content to have the color of his skin changed, and stand in his place? Who among us would then be content with the counsels of patience and delay?

The old code of equity law under which we live commands for every wrong a remedy, but in too many communities, in too many parts of the country, wrongs are inflicted on Negro citizens for which there are no remedies at law. Unless the Congress acts, their only remedy is in the streets.

Television Address
June 11, 1963

Nuclear Power

We should be able to persuade friend and foe alike that continued neglect of this problem [nuclear tests] will make all the world a loser—while its solution will make all the world a winner—and a better place with a better future for the children of every land.

Portland, Oregon
August 1, 1959

We must be prepared in this nation to fight an all-out nuclear war—or else we cannot deter an all-out nuclear attack upon us.

Lake Charles, Louisiana
October 16, 1959

Even little wars are dangerous in this nuclear world.

Address to Protestant Council of New York
New York City
November 8, 1963

The door is open for the nuclear defense of . . . [NATO] to become a source of confidence, instead of a cause of contention.

State of the Union Message
January 14, 1963

We will not act prematurely or unnecessarily risk the costs of world-wide nuclear war in which even the fruits of victory would be ashes in our mouth. But neither will we shrink from that risk at any time it must be faced.

Television Address
October 22, 1962

[101]

Opportunity

When written in Chinese, the word "crisis" is composed of two characters—one represents danger and the other represents opportunity.

United Negro College Fund Convocation
Indianapolis, Indiana
April 12, 1959

Equal housing opportunities are of little avail if only slums are available.

National Civil Liberties Conference
Washington, D.C.
April 16, 1959

We have not only obligations to fulfill; we have great opportunities to realize.

Message to Congress
March 22, 1961

We are not developing the nation's wealth for its own sake. Wealth is the means, and people are the ends. All our material riches will avail us little if we do not use them to expand the opportunities of our people.

If this nation is to grow in wisdom and strength, then every able high school graduate should have the opportunity to develop his talents.

State of the Union Message
January 11, 1962

Does every American boy and girl have an opportunity to develop whatever talents he or she has? All of us do not have equal talent, but all of us should have an equal opportunity to develop our talents.

San Diego State College
San Diego, California
June 6, 1963

Peace

The condition for the freedom of the still captive peoples—*is* peace.

Pulaski Day Dinner
Milwaukee, Wisconsin
October 17, 1959

Where nature makes natural allies of us all, we can demonstrate that beneficial relations are possible even with those with whom we most deeply disagree —and this must someday be the basis of world peace and world law.

State of the Union Message
January 29, 1961

While we are ready to defend our interests, we shall also be ready to search for peace. . . .

Report to the People
July 25, 1961

Let no man of peace despair. For he does not stand alone.

Peace is not solely a matter of military or technical problems; it is primarily a problem of politics and people.

It is . . . our intention to challenge the Soviet Union, not to an arms race, but to a peace race: to advance with us step by step, stage by stage, until general and complete disarmament has actually been achieved. We invite them now to go beyond agreement in principle to reach agreement on actual plans.

Let us call a truce to terror. Let us invoke the blessings of peace. And, as we build an international capacity to keep peace, let us join in dismantling the national capacity to wage war.

United Nations
September 25, 1961

There is no way to maintain the frontiers of freedom without cost and commitment and risk. There is no swift and easy path to peace in our generation.

Veterans Day
Arlington National Cemetery
November 11, 1961

Peace and freedom do not come cheap, and we are destined, all of us here today, to live out most—if not all—of our lives in uncertainty and challenge and peril. . . .

University of North Carolina
Chapel Hill, North Carolina
November, 1961

Our preparations for war will bring us preservation of peace.

Television Address
March 2, 1962

Our goal is not the victory of might, but the vindication of right; not peace at the expense of freedom, but both peace *and* freedom. . . .

Television Address
October 22, 1962

While we shall never weary in the defense of freedom, neither shall we abandon the pursuit of peace.

The mere absence of war is not peace. . . . A moment of pause is not a promise of peace.

State of the Union Message
January 14, 1963

We are unwilling to impose our system on any unwilling people, but we are willing and able to engage in peaceful competition with any people on earth.

Genuine peace must be the product of many nations, the sum of many acts. It must be dynamic, not static, changing to meet the challenge of each new generation. For peace is a process, a way of solving problems.

I have . . . chosen this time and place to discuss a topic on which ignorance too often abounds and truth is too rarely perceived—yet it is the most important topic on earth: world peace.

What kind of peace do I mean? What kind of peace do we seek? Not a Pax Americana enforced on the world by American weapons of war. Not the peace of the grave or the security of the slave. I am talking about genuine peace, the kind of peace that makes life on earth worth living, the kind that enables men and nations to grow and to hope and to build a better life for their children—not merely peace for Americans, but peace for all men and women; not merely peace in our time, but peace for all time.

The American University
Washington, D.C.
June 10, 1963

We have no illusions now that there are short cuts on the road to peace.

Television Address
July 26, 1963

Peace is a daily, a weekly, a monthly process, gradually changing opinions, slowly eroding old barriers, quietly building new structures. And however undramatic the pursuit of peace, that pursuit must go on.

[106]

A test ban treaty is a milestone, but it is not the millennium.

The long labor of peace is an undertaking for every nation, and in this effort none of us can remain unaligned. To this goal none can be uncommitted.

United Nations
September 20, 1963

While maintaining our readiness for war, let us exhaust every avenue for peace.

University of Maine
Orono, Maine
October 19, 1963

Peace Corps

A pool of trained American men and women sent overseas by the U.S. Government or through private organizations and institutions to help foreign countries meet their urgent needs for skilled manpower.

Message to Congress
March 1, 1961

We have in this country, an immense reservoir of . . . men and women anxious to sacrifice their energies and time and toil to the cause of world peace and human progress.

Life in the Peace Corps will not be easy. . . . But if life will not be easy, it will be rich and satisfying. For every young American who participates in the Peace Corps—who works in foreign lands—will know that he or she is sharing in the great common task of bringing to men that decent way of life which is the foundation of freedom and a condition of peace.

Statement Establishing the Peace Corps
March 1, 1961

Physical Fitness

Do your children go every week and watch a basketball game, or do they do something to make themselves fit? I think we are inclined to think that if we watch a football game or a baseball game, we have taken part in it.

Interview with Dave Garroway
January 31, 1961

The ability to afford adequate health care is to no avail without adequate health facilities.

The health of our nation is a key to its future—to its economic vitality, to the morale and efficiency of its citizens, to our success in achieving our own goals and demonstrating to others the benefits of a free society.

Message to Congress
February 9, 1961

We do not want in the United States a nation of spectators. We want a nation of participants in the vigorous life.

Youth Fitness Conference
February 21, 1961

What we must do is literally change the physical habits of millions of Americans; and that is far more difficult than changing their tastes, their fashions, or even their politics.

We are under-exercised as a nation. We look instead of play. We ride instead of walk. Our existence deprives us of the minimum of physical activity essential for healthy living.

National Football Foundation
New York City
December 5, 1961

Politics

In this great free society of ours, both of our parties —the Republican and the Democratic parties—serve the interests of the people.

Meeting of the Democratic National Committee
January 21, 1961

Our political life is becoming so expensive, so mechanized and so dominated by professional politicians and public relations men that the idealist who dreams of independent statesmanship is rudely awakened by the necessities of election and accomplishment.

Profiles in Courage
(Young Readers Edition)

Poverty

We cannot win . . . hearts by making . . . [others] dependent upon our handouts.

Washington, D.C.
July 2, 1957

The world may be enjoying more prosperity than ever before—but . . . it has never seen so much poverty in all its history.

Seattle, Washington
June 20, 1959

American agricultural abundance can be forged into both a significant instrument of foreign policy and a weapon against domestic hardship and hunger.

Abundant production has filled our bins and warehouses, but one out of ten American households has a diet so inadequate that it falls below two-thirds of the standard nutrition requirements.

Message to Congress
March 16, 1961

If a free society cannot help the many who are poor, it cannot save the few who are rich.

Inaugural Address
January 20, 1961

Political sovereignty is but a mockery without the means to meet poverty and illiteracy and disease.

United Nations
September 25, 1961

So long as freedom from hunger is only half achieved, so long as two thirds of the nations have food deficits, no citizen, no nation, can afford to be satisfied. We have the ability, as members of the human race, we have the means, we have the capacity, to eliminate hunger from the face of the earth in our lifetime.

World Food Congress
Washington, D.C.
June 4, 1963

Preparedness

A boxer cannot work himself into proper psychological and physical condition for a fight that he seriously believes will never come off.

We cannot tell anyone to keep out of our hemisphere unless our armaments and *the people behind*

[111]

these armaments are prepared to back up the command, even to the ultimate point of going to war.

Why England Slept

To sound the alarm is not to panic—it is not to sell America short.

Washington, D.C.
August 14, 1958

To preserve, we must extend.

Washington University
Lincoln, Nebraska
October 13, 1959

Piecemeal projects, hastily designed to match the rhythm of the fiscal year, are no substitute for orderly long-term planning . . .

Message to Congress
March 22, 1961

Our preparation against danger is our hope of safety.

State of the Union Message
March 28, 1961

Diplomacy and defense are no longer distinct alternatives, one to be used where the other fails; each must complement the other.

Message to Congress
March 28, 1961

The time to repair the roof is when the sun is shining.

State of the Union Message
January 11, 1962

[The] task must begin at home. For if we cannot fulfill our own ideals here, we cannot expect others to accept them. And when the youngest child alive today has grown to the cares of manhood, our position in the world will be determined first of all by what provisions we make today—for his education, his health, and his opportunities for a good home and a good job and a good life.

State of the Union Message
January 11, 1962

We will not prematurely or unnecessarily risk the costs of world-wide nuclear war in which even the fruits of victory would be ashes in our mouth, but neither will we shrink from that risk at any time it must be faced.

Television Address
October 22, 1962

If we do not plan today for the future growth of . . . our great natural assets—not only parks and forests, but wildlife and wilderness preserves and water projects of all kinds—our children and their children will be poorer in every sense of the word.

State of the Union Message
January 14, 1963

We seek a relaxation of tensions without relaxing our guard.

The American University
Washington, D.C.
June 10, 1963

Abraham Lincoln, in the dark days before the Civil War in my own country said, "I know there is a God. I see a storm coming. If He has a part and a place for me, then I am ready." No one can tell in the future whether there is a storm coming for all of us, but whatever happens, we believe in God and we are ready.

Frankfurt, West Germany
June 25, 1963

Where 180 million Americans now live, by the year 2000 there will be 350 million of them, and we have to provide for them, as Theodore Roosevelt and Franklin Roosevelt and the others provided for us.

Ashland, Wisconsin
September 24, 1963

Marshal Lyautey, who was the great French marshal in North Africa, was once talking to his gardener, and he suggested that he plant a tree, and the

gardener said, "Well, why plant it? It won't flower
for a hundred years." And Marshal Lyautey said,
"In that case, plant it this afternoon."

University of North Dakota
Grand Forks, North Dakota
September 25, 1963

Progress

The means are at hand with which to make . . . a
better life.

Washington, D.C.
January 1, 1959

Political freedom is the precondition to economic
and social development.

Africa is undergoing an agricultural, industrial,
technological, urban, social and political revolution
. . . passing from a feudal . . . stage into the atomic
age in a matter of decades. It is recapitulating the
history of the last five centuries of European society
in fifty years.

In Africa we see more than Africa. We see there
a continent so long "behind God's back" coming into
its own. We see two hundred million human beings
awakening from centuries of sleep. We see the ideas

[115]

of freedom being reborn. We see the birth pangs of independence being suffered anew. We see the problems of national development, of modern civilization, weighing down the shoulders of a new generation. We see, above all, the image of modern man being created in a vast new land under new and difficult conditions.

Conference of American Society of African Culture
New York City
June 28, 1959

Only an effort of towering dimensions can insure fulfillment of our plan for a decade of progress.

We have the capacity to strike off the remaining bonds of poverty and ignorance, to free our people for the spiritual and intellectual fulfillment which has always been the goal of our civilization.

The best road to progress is freedom's road.

Social progress is not a substitute for economic development. It is an effort to create a social framework within which all the people of a nation can share in the benefits of prosperity and participate in the process of growth. Economic growth without social progress lets the great majority of the people remain in poverty, while a privileged few reap the benefits of rising abundance.

Message to Congress
March 14, 1961

Our security and progress cannot be cheaply purchased; and their price must be found in what we all forego as well as what we all must pay.

Message to Congress
May 25, 1961

Unless man can match his strides in weaponry and technology with equal strides in social and political development, our great strength, like that of the dinosaur, will become incapable of proper control, and man, like the dinosaur, will vanish from the earth.

United Nations
September 25, 1961

Purpose

The old American purposes are still wholly relevant. What this generation must do is to face its problems—at home and abroad. They cannot be divided.

[117]

PURPOSE

The American purpose remains what it has been since the nation's founding: to demonstrate that the organization of men and societies on the basis of human freedom is not an absurdity, but an enriching, ennobling, practical achievement.

So long as there are slums in which people have to live, so long as there are schools that are overcrowded or antiquated or inadequate, so long as there are men in search of decent jobs and homes, so long as there are sick people in need of medical care, so long as anyone suffers discrimination by reason of color, race, religion, or national origin, the work of America is not done.

Washington, D.C.
January 1, 1960

A balanced federal program must go well beyond incentives for investment in plant and equipment. It must include equally determined measures to invest in human beings . . .

Message to Congress
February 20, 1961

This is our guide for the present and our vision for the future: a free community of nations, independent but interdependent, uniting north and south, east and west, in one great family of man, outgrowing and transcending the hates and fears that rend our age.

We will not reach that goal today, or tomorrow. We may not reach it in our own lifetime. But the quest is the greatest adventure of our century. We sometimes chafe at the burden of our obligations, the complexity of our decisions, the agony of our choices. But there is no comfort or security for us in evasion, no solution in abdication, no relief in irresponsibility.

Our basic goal remains the same: a peaceful world community of free and independent states, free to choose their own future and their own system, so long as it does not threaten the freedom of others.

State of the Union Message
January 11, 1962

We can move forward with the confidence that is born of success and the skill that is born of experience. And as we move, let us take heart from the certainty that we are united not only by danger and necessity, but by hope and purpose as well.

We are called to a great new mission ... to create a new social order, founded on liberty and justice, in which men are the masters of their fate, in which states are the servants of their citizens, and in which all men and women can share a better life for themselves and their children.

Frankfurt, West Germany
June 25, 1963

Religion

This country has been singularly blessed in its ability to take the best of all religions and cultures—not merely tolerating differences but building a new, richer life upon them.

Washington, D.C.
1960

Religious freedom and religious conviction are the two hallmarks of American society.

No man who enters the office to which I have succeeded can fail to recognize how every President of the United States has placed special reliance on his faith in God. Every President has taken comfort and courage when told . . . that the Lord "will be with thee. He will not fail thee nor forsake thee. Fear not, neither be thou dismayed."

Dedication Breakfast of the
International Christian Leadership
Washington, D.C.
February 9, 1961

[120]

Religious Freedom

The search for freedom of worship has brought people to America from the days of the Pilgrims to modern times.

The very diversity of religious belief has made for religious toleration. In demanding freedom for itself, each sect had increasingly to permit freedom for others.

People who gambled their lives on the right to believe in their own God would not lightly surrender that right in a new society.

A Nation of Immigrants

No one can be forced to be devout by being forced to swear that he does not believe in the locally unpopular religion.

Washington, D.C.
June 29, 1959

What church I go to on Sunday, what dogma of the Catholic Church I believe in, is my business, and whatever faith any other American has is his business.

Washington, D.C.
1960

[121]

RESPONSIBILITY

This country was founded by men and women who were dedicated or came to be dedicated to two propositions: first, a strong religious conviction, and secondly, a recognition that this conviction could flourish only under a system of freedom.

I think it is appropriate that we pay tribute to this great constitutional principle, which is enshrined in the First Amendment of the Constitution: the principle of religious independence, of religious liberty, of religious freedom. But I think it is also important that we pay tribute to and acknowledge another great principle, and that is the principle of religious conviction.

Religious freedom has no significance unless it is accomplished by conviction.

We cannot have religious freedom without political freedom . . .

Dedication Breakfast of the
International Christian Leadership
February 9, 1961

Responsibility

The cost of doing the job right is not more than we can afford. It may not be cheap or easy or popular —but we cannot afford to do less.

Washington, D.C.
February 19, 1959

Our hopes for relaxation are high. But the hard facts of the matter are that we . . . cannot escape our dangers by recoiling from them—or by being lulled to sleep.

University of Rochester
Rochester, New York
October 1, 1959

Of those to whom much is given, much is required.

Massachusetts State Legislature
January 9, 1961

The prudent heir takes careful inventory of his legacies, and gives a faithful accounting to those whom he owes an obligation of trust.

State of the Union Message
January 29, 1961

The efforts of governments alone will never be enough. In the end, the people must choose and the people must help themselves.

Reception for Latin-American Diplomats
Washington, D.C.
March 13, 1961

At a time when a single clash could escalate overnight into a holocaust of mushroom clouds, a great power does not prove its firmness by leaving the task of exploring the other's intentions to sentries or those without full responsibility.

University of Washington
Seattle, Washington
November 16, 1961

The world's prognosis prescribes . . . not a year's vacation for us, but a year of obligation and opportunity.

State of the Union Message
January 14, 1963

We have a great obligation . . . to use whatever time remains to prevent the spread of nuclear weapons . . .

Television Address
July 26, 1963

Never before has man had such capacity to control his own environment—to end thirst and hunger, to conquer poverty and disease, to banish illiteracy and massive human misery. We have the power to make this the best generation of mankind in the history of the world, or to make it the last.

The United States . . . does have a special responsibility in the world. It is in fact, a threefold responsibility: a responsibility to our citizens, a responsibility to the people of the whole world who are affected by our decisions, and to the next generation of humanity.

United Nations
September 20, 1963

Our privileges can be no greater than our obligations. The protection of our rights can endure no longer than the performance of our responsibilities.

Vanderbilt University
Nashville, Tennessee
1963

Revolution

At least seven peaceful revolutions are rocking our nation and our world: . . . the revolution in population . . . the revolution on the farm . . . the revolution of technology and energy—the wonders of automation and atomization . . . the revolution in the standard of living . . . the revolution in weapons development in the field of national security . . . the revolution in the underdeveloped nations of the world . . . the revolution of nationalism.

Seattle, Washington
June 20, 1959

[125]

Rights

The *Risorgimento* which gave birth to modern Italy, like the American Revolution which led to the birth of our country, was the re-awakening of the most deeply-held ideals of Western Civilization: the desire for freedom, and protection of the rights of the individual. . . . The state exists for the protection of those rights, and those rights do not come to us because of the generosity of the state.

> Observance of Centennial of Italian Unification
> Washington, D.C.
> March 16, 1961

The right of free choice is no special privilege. . . . It is an elemental requirement of human justice.

> West Berlin
> June 26, 1963

Every American has the right to a decent life for himself and a better life for his children.

> Inter-American Press Association
> Miami Beach, Florida
> November 18, 1963

Science

The expanding wonders of science . . . have captured man's imagination, challenged the powers of his mind, and given him the tools for rapid progress.

Reception for Latin-American Diplomats
Washington, D.C.
March 13, 1961

If scientific discovery has not been an unalloyed blessing, if it has conferred on mankind the power not only to create but also to annihilate, it has at the same time provided humanity with a supreme challenge and a supreme testing. If the challenge and the testing are too much for humanity, then we are all doomed; but I believe that the future can be bright, and I believe that it can be certain. Man is still the master of his own fate, and I believe that the power of science and the responsibility of science have offered mankind a new opportunity not only for intellectual growth, but for moral discipline, not only for the acquisition of knowledge but for the strengthening of our nerve and will.

Every time . . . scientists make a major invention . . . politicians have to invent a new institution to cope with it, and almost invariably these days, and happily, it must be an international institution.

National Academy of Sciences
Washington, D.C.
October 22, 1963

Research in space medicine holds the promise of substantial benefit for those of us who are earthbound, for our effort in space is not, as some have suggested, a competitor for the natural resources that we need to develop the earth. It is a working partner and co-producer of these resources. And nothing makes this clearer than the fact that medicine in space is going to make our lives healthier and happier here on earth.

Aero-Space Medical Health Center
Brooks Air Force Base, Texas
November 21, 1963

Security

As we look at the world, however imperfect it may be, however frustrating it may be, however limited our authority may be on occasions, however impossible we may find it to have our writ accepted, nevertheless, the United States is secure, it is at peace, and a good many dozens of countries are secure because of us.

University of Minnesota
September 24, 1963

Space Age

The exploration of space is an action of science and of human adventure.

> Palm Beach, Florida
> December 15, 1959

Peace in space will help us naught once peace on earth is gone.

> State of the Union Message
> January 11, 1962

Space is open to us now; and our eagerness to share its meaning is not governed by the efforts of others. We go into space because whatever mankind must undertake, free men must fully share.

While we cannot guarantee that we shall one day be first [in space], we can guarantee that any failure to make the effort will make us last.

> Message to Congress
> May 25, 1961

We choose to go to the moon in this decade and do other things, not because they are easy, but because they are hard . . .

There is no strife, no prejudice, no national conflict in outer space as yet. Its hazards are hostile to us all. Its conquest deserves the best of all mankind, and its opportunity for peaceful cooperation may never come again.

The opening vistas of space promise high costs and hardships, as well as high reward.

Space can be explored and mastered without feeding the fires of war . . . without repeating the mistakes that man has made in extending his writ around this globe of ours.

Those who came before us made certain that this country rode the first waves of the industrial revolution, the first waves of modern invention and the first wave of nuclear power, and this generation does not intend to flounder in the backwash of the coming age of space. We mean to be part of it. We mean to lead it, for the eyes of the world now look into space, to the moon and to the planets beyond; and we have vowed that we shall not see it governed by a hostile flag of conquest, but by a banner of freedom and peace. We have vowed that we shall not see space filled with weapons of mass destruction, but with instruments of knowledge and understanding.

Rice University
Houston, Texas
September 12, 1962

Frank O'Connor, the Irish writer, tells in one of his books how, as a boy, he and his friends would make their way across the countryside. And when they came to an orchard wall that seemed too high and too doubtful to try, and too difficult to permit their voyage to continue, they took off their hats and tossed them over the wall—and then they had no choice but to follow them. This nation has tossed its cap over the wall of space—and we have no choice but to follow it.

Aero-Space Medical Health Center
Brooks Air Force Base, Texas
November 21, 1963

Strength

Any system of government will work when everything is going well. It's the system that functions in the pinches that survives.

Why England Slept

This nation can afford to be strong; it cannot afford to be weak.

Message to Congress
March 28, 1961

We need to strengthen our nation by investing in our youth. . . we need to strengthen our nation by safeguarding its health. . . we need to strengthen our na-

tion by protecting the basic rights of its citizens. . .
we need to strengthen our nation by making the best
and most economical use of its resources and facilities.

State of the Union Message
January 14, 1963

Survival

We have completely failed to understand the crucial
importance of intellectual achievements in the race
for security and survival.

Loyola College Alumni Banquet
Baltimore, Maryland
February 18, 1958

Ancient man survived the more powerful beasts
about him because his wisdom—his strategy and his
policies—overcame his lack of power. We can do the
same. We dare not attempt less . . .

Senate Address
August 14, 1958

Irrational barriers and ancient prejudices fall
quickly when the question of survival itself is at stake.

United Negro College Fund Convocation
Indianapolis, Indiana
April 12, 1959

We have not made as concentrated an effort on techniques for preserving mankind as we have on techniques of destruction.

University of California
Los Angeles, California
November 2, 1959

No sane society chooses to commit national suicide.

Washington, D.C.
December 11, 1959

The next year, the next decade, in all likelihood the next generation, will require more bravery, and wisdom on our part than any period in our history. We will be face to face, every day, in every part of our lives and times, with the real issue of our age—the issue of survival.

Washington, D.C.
1960

Only the strong, only the industrious, only the determined, only the courageous, only the visionary who determines the real nature of our struggle, can possibly survive.

American Society of Newspaper Editors
Washington, D.C.
April 20, 1961

Our deep spiritual confidence that this nation will survive the perils of today . . . compels us to invest in our nation's future, to consider and meet our obliga-

tions to our children and the numberless generations
that will follow.

Message to Congress
March 1, 1962

Suspicion

Suspicion on one side breeds suspicion on the other,
and new weapons beget counterweapons.

The American University
Washington, D.C.
June 10, 1963

Taxes

Expense-account living has become a byword. . . .
The slogan, "It's deductible," should pass from our
scene.

A strong and sound federal tax system is essential
to America's future.

Message to Congress
April 20, 1961

It is a paradoxical truth that tax rates are too high
today and tax revenues are too low, and the soundest

way to raise revenues in the long run is to cut rates now.

Economic Club of New York
New York City
December 14, 1962

United Nations

Never have the nations of the world had so much to lose or so much to gain. Together we shall save our planet or together we shall perish in its flames. Save it we can, and save it we must, and then shall we earn the eternal thanks of mankind and, as peacemakers, the eternal blessing of God.

Until all the powerful are just, the weak will be secure only in the strength of this Assembly.

The great question . . . is still before us: whether man's cherished hopes for progress and freedom are to be destroyed by terror and disruption; whether the "four winds of war" can be tamed in time to free the cooling winds of reason; and whether the pledges of our Charter are to be fulfilled or defined—pledges to secure peace, progress, human rights and world law.

[The United Nations] will either grow to meet the challenge of our age, or it will be gone with the wind, without influence, without force, without respect. Were we to let it die, to enfeeble its vigor, to cripple its power, we would condemn the future.

Already the United Nations has become both the measure and the vehicle of man's most generous impulses. Already it has provided ... a means to holding violence within bounds.

United Nations
September 25, 1961

Our instrument and our hope is the United Nations, and I see little merit in the impatience of those who would abandon this imperfect world instrument because they dislike our imperfect world. For the troubles of a world organization merely reflect the troubles of the world itself. And if the organization is weakened, these troubles can only increase.

This is our guide for the present and our vision for the future: a free community of nations, independent but interdependent, uniting north and south, east and west, in one great family of man, outgrowing and transcending the hates and fears that rend our age.

We will not reach that goal today, or tomorrow. We may not reach it in our own lifetime. But the quest is the greatest adventure of our century.

State of the Union Message
January 11, 1962

The wave of the future is not the conquest of the world by a single domestic creed, but the liberation of the diverse energies of free nations and free men.

> University of California
> Berkeley, California
> March 23, 1962

Acting on our own by ourselves, we cannot establish justice throughout the world. We cannot insure its domestic tranquillity, or provide for its common defense, or promote its general welfare, or secure the blessings of liberty to ourselves and our posterity. But joined with other free nations, we can do all this and more.

> Independence Hall
> Philadelphia, Pennsylvania
> July 4, 1962

The ocean, the atmosphere, outer space, belong not to one nation, or one ideology, but to all mankind.

> National Academy of Sciences
> Washington, D.C.
> October 22, 1963

Let us take our stand here in this assembly of nations. And let us see if we, in our own time, can move the world to a just and lasting peace.

The effort to improve the conditions of man, however, is not a task for the few. It is the task of all nations, acting alone, acting in groups, acting in the

United Nations; for plague and pestilence, and plunder and pollution, the hazards of nature and the hunger of children, are the foes of every nation. The earth, the sea and the air are the concern of every nation. And science, technology and education can be the allies of every nation.

We are opposed to *apartheid* and all forms of human oppression. We do not advocate the rights of black Africans in order to drive out white Africans. Our concern is the right of all men to equal protection under the law; and since human rights are indivisible, this body cannot stand aside when those rights are abused and neglected by any member state.

United Nations
September 20, 1963

Vote

In a free society, those with the power to govern are necessarily responsive to those with the right to vote.

The right to vote in a free American election is the most powerful and precious right in the world, and it must not be denied on the ground of race or color.

Message to Congress
February 28, 1963

War

Many of the old conceptions of war and peace, friend and foe, victory and defeat, must be reshaped in the light of new realities.

Foreign Affairs
October, 1957

We do not want to fight, but we have fought before.

Gun battles are caused by outlaws, and not by officers of the peace.

Report to the People
July 25, 1961

The world was not meant to be a prison in which man awaits his execution. Nor has mankind survived the tests and trials of thousands of years to surrender everything, including its existence, now.

State of the Union Message
January 11, 1962

So let us persevere. Peace need not be impracticable, and war need not be inevitable.

The American University
Washington, D.C.
June 10, 1963

Since the beginning of history, war has been mankind's constant companion.

Television Address
July 26, 1963

Witticisms

Several nights ago, I dreamed that the good Lord touched me on the shoulder and said, "Don't worry, you'll be the Democratic presidential nominee in 1960. What's more, you'll be elected." I told Stu Symington about my dream. "Funny thing," said Stu, "I had the same dream myself."

We both told our dreams to Lyndon Johnson, and Johnson said, "That's funny. For the life of me, I can't remember tapping either of you two boys for the job."

1958 Campaign

Question: Senator, you were promised military intelligence briefing from the President. Have you received that?

Mr. Kennedy: Yes. I talked on Thursday morning to General Wheeler from the Defense Department.

Question: What was his first name?

Mr. Kennedy: He didn't brief me on that.

Press Conference
Anchorage, Alaska
September 4, 1960

I want to express my appreciation to the Governor. Every time he introduces me as the potentially greatest President in the history of the United States, I always think perhaps he is overstating it one or two degrees. George Washington wasn't a bad President, and I do want to say a word for Thomas Jefferson. But, otherwise, I will accept the compliment.

Muskegon, Michigan
September 5, 1960

We had an interesting convention at Los Angeles, and we ended with a strong Democratic platform which we called "The Rights of Man." The Republican platform has also been presented. I do not know its title, but it has been referred to as "The Power of Positive Thinking."

New York City
September 14, 1960

I know something about Mr. Khrushchev, whom I met a year ago in the Senate Foreign Relations Committee, and I know something about the nature and history of his country, which I visited in 1939.

Mr. Khrushchev himself, it is said, told the story a few years ago about the Russian who began to run through the Kremlin, shouting, "Khrushchev is a fool. Khrushchev is a fool." He was sentenced, the Premier said, to twenty-three years in prison, "three for insulting the party secretary, and twenty for revealing a state secret."

Pikesville, Maryland
September 16, 1960

I have sent him [former President Harry S. Truman] the following wire: "Dear Mr. President: I have noted with interest your suggestion as to where those who vote for my opponent should go. While I understand and sympathize with your deep motivation, I think it is important that our side try to refrain from raising the religious issue."

Alfred E. Smith Memorial Dinner
New York City
October 19, 1960

This isn't the way they told me it was when I first decided to run for the Presidency. After reading about the schedules of the President, I thought we all stayed in bed until ten or eleven and then got out and drove around.

Rockford, Illinois
October 24, 1960

This state knows the issues of this campaign—Senior Citizens. Senator McNamara is chairman of the Senate Committee on Senior Citizens. I am vice chairman. We are both aging fast.

Warren, Michigan
October 26, 1960

Ladies and gentlemen, the outstanding news story of this week was not [about] the events of the United Nations, or even the Presidential campaign. It was a story coming out of my own city of Boston that Ted Williams of the Boston Red Sox had retired from baseball. It seems that at forty-two he was too old. It shows that perhaps experience isn't enough.

Minneapolis, Minnesota
October, 1960

A dilemma, it seems to me, is posed by the occasion of a Presidential address to a business group on business conditions less than four weeks after entering the White House, for it is too early to be claiming credit for the new Administration and too late to be blaming the old one.

National Industrial Conference Board
Washington, D.C.
February 13, 1961

When we got into office, the thing that surprised me most was to find that things were just as bad as we'd been saying they were.

Dinner on the President's Birthday
May 27, 1961

Speaking of jobs for relatives, Master Robert Kennedy, who is four, came to see me today, but I told him we already had an Attorney General.

[143]

I had plenty of problems when I came in, but wait until the fellow that follows me sees what he will inherit.

National Security Council Meeting

"Caroline," the President shouted, "have you been eating candy?"

There was no answer from the President's young daughter.

"Caroline," the President repeated, "have you been eating candy? Answer, yes, no, or maybe."

It has recently been suggested that whether I serve one or two terms in the Presidency, I will find myself, at the end of that period, at what might be called the awkward age, too old to begin a new career and too young to write my memoirs.

Address to the National Industrial Conference Board
Washington, D.C.
February 13, 1961

The Catholic, Protestant, and Jewish clergy are entitled to their views. I think it is quite appropriate that they should not change their views merely because of the religion of the occupant of the White House.

Press Conference
March 15, 1961

This city is no stranger to me. A Parisian designed the city of Washington. He laid out our broad boulevards after living here in this community. When he had finished his generous designs, he presented a bill to the Congress for ninety thousand dollars, and the Congress of the United States, in one of those bursts of economic fervor for which they are justifiably famous awarded him the munificent sum of three thousand dollars. Some people have been so unkind as to suggest that your clothes designers have been collecting his bill ever since.

Paris
1961

Politics is an astonishing profession. It has enabled me to go from being an obscure member of the junior varsity at Harvard to being an honorary member of the Football Hall of Fame.

National Football Foundation Dinner
New York City
December, 1961

Chancellor Adenauer was generous enough to say that the outpouring was spontaneous, and I do believe that there was spontaneous good will. But I cannot believe all of those flags they held in their hands came from their rooms and from their houses. As an old politician, somebody must have been working, Mr. Chancellor.

Bonn, West Germany
June 23, 1963

[145]

I don't want to give the impression that every member of this Administration in Washington is Irish. It just seems that way.

City Hall
Cork, Ireland
June 28, 1963

As all of you know, some circles invented the myth that after Al Smith's defeat in 1928, he sent a one-word telegram to the Pope: "Unpack."

After my press conference on the school bill, I received a one-word wire from the Pope: "Pack."

Speaking of the religious issue, I asked the Chief Justice tonight whether he thought our new education bill was constitutional and he said, "It's clearly constitutional—it hasn't a prayer."

Gridiron Club
Washington, D.C.

Index

A

a better life, all men and women can share, 119

The means are at hand to make, 41, 115

abdication, no solution in, 119

abroad, judged more by what we do at home than by what we preach, 18

abundance, the gap between, here and near-starvation abroad, 63

Action, 15–18

and foresight are, preludes to freedom, 15

creative, determined, 17

every effort to test our hopes by, 18

from an aroused public, 15

no point in calling for vigorous, 17

actions, from words to, 18

Adenauer, Konrad, 145

Administration, too early to be claiming credit for the new, 143

adversaries, I do not believe our, are tired, 20

adversary's moves, time to stop reacting to our, 15

adversity, partners in, 37

advice, that ultimate luxury, free, 17

afford, we cannot, to do less, 122

Africa, is undergoing, revolution, 115

African leaders, It was in our schools that, the most renowned,

learned, 54

aggression, We shall neither commit nor provoke, 48

aggressor, potential, must know that our response will be suitable, selective, swift and effective, 16

agricultural abundance, instrument of foreign policy, 110

agriculture be not only progressive but prosperous, 63

Alliance for Progress, 64, 89–90

allies, if we and our, were to believe, 37

necessity has made us, 25

Where nature makes natural, 103

alone, no man of peace ((stands)), 104

no nation can build its destiny, 37

we are not, 19

America, an, which practices what it preaches, 83

ask not what, will do for you, 66

A strong, depends on its cities, 31

freedom of worship has brought people to, 121

it is not to sell, short, 112

name, was given to this continent, 35

stands for progress in human rights, 60

The cause of all mankind is the cause of, 19

the work of, is not done, 118

America and Americans, 19–20

"a heterogeneous race but a homogeneous nation," 35

INDEX

INDEX

INDEX

INDEX

mass extermination, in the age of, 91

masters, not the victims, of our history, 50

Mayflower, 78

medicine in space is going to make our lives healthier and happier here on earth, 128

men are masters of their fate, 119

they have the talent to put those, back to work, 58

We need, who can dream, 77

men's minds, It takes time to change, 76

Middle East is a monument to Western misunderstanding, 87

military establishment, the permanent maintenance of a large, 21–22

military intelligence briefing, you were promised, 140

military solution, problems facing the world today are not susceptible to a, 22

missiles are only minutes away, 21

moon, We choose to go to the, 129

moral standards of a society, 82

Moslem, a, can serve in the Israeli Parliament, 27

myth, The great enemy of the truth, not the lie—but the, 33

N

nation, "a heterogeneous race but a homogeneous," 35

can be no stronger abroad than she is at home, 83

conceived in revolution, 81

image to the world as a, 31

matured in independence, 81

must move fast even to stand still, 18

neglect our cities, we neglect the, 31

nurtured in liberty, 81

Our progress as a, 55

This, can afford to be strong; it cannot afford to be weak, 131

This, raised in freedom, 48

This, was born of revolution, 48

this, will survive, 133

We are under-exercised as a, 109

We need to strengthen our, 131–132

nationalism, the revolution of, 125

nations, Never have the, of the world had so much to lose or so much to gain, 135

nation's psychology, it takes violent shocks to change an entire, 76

natural assets, future growth of . . . our great, 113

Natural Resources, 95–98

Our future greatness and our strength depend upon, 95

necessity has made us allies, 25

negotiable, What's mine is mine and what's your is, 83

negotiate, we shall never, out of fear, 49

Negro has about half as much chance to get through college, 98

Only in the case of the, has the melting pot failed, 98

retained his loyalty, 99

working as a messenger, 99

Negroes, 98–100

no second-class citizens except, 99

nuclear defense, The door is open for the, of, 101

Nuclear Power, 100–101

((nuclear tests)), continued neglect of this problem, 100

nuclear war, We must be prepared, to fight an all-out, 101

We will not risk the costs of world-wide, 101, 113

nuclear weapons, We have a great obligation . . . to prevent the spread of, 124

nuclear world, Even little wars are dangerous in this, 101

O

oath, nothing takes precedence over his, 30

oath of office, above my conscience, 27

obligation, a year of, and opportunity, 124

We have a great, 124

V

Vatican, opposed to appointment of an ambassador to the, 26

victory, fruits of, would be ashes in our mouth, 101, 113
not the, of might, 105
not, of one nation, but, of men, 36

Vinci, Leonardo da, 94

violence, a means to holding, within bounds, 136

visionaries, We are all, 72

Vote, 138

W

War, 139–140
absence of, is not peace, 105
"four winds of," 135
has been mankind's constant companion, 140
need not be inevitable, 139
Our preparations for, will bring us preservation of peace, 105
primary purpose of our arms is peace, not, 21
readiness for, 107
scourge of, 33–34
the people don't want to go to, 44
weapons of, must be abolished, 50
we think not of, but of peace, 80

Washington, ((D.C.)), A Parisian designed the city of, 145

Washington, George, 141

way of living, right and proper to support vigorously our, 38

weak, If we are, words will be of no help, 50
This nation, cannot afford to be, 131

weakness, Civility is not a sign of, 81
Men no longer pretend that the quest for disarmament is a sign of, 50
not a confession of, but a statement of strength, 21

weaknesses, democracy must recognize its, 44

not right and proper to be blind to its, 38

Wealth is the means, and people are the ends, 102

weapons, new, beget counterweapons, 134

weapons development, the revolution in, 125

weapons of war must be abolished, 50

Wells, H. G., 55

Witticisms, 140–146

words cannot construct an alliance, 43
from, to actions, 18
must offer deeds, not, 42
need merely to convey conviction, not belligerence, 50

work, machines that put men out of, 58
there is only hard, 15
the, of America is not done, 118

world, a, we did not make, 68
Every American is now involved in the, 19
our position in the, 113
reap the kind of, we deserve, 18
the problems facing the, today are not susceptible to a military solution, 22
The, was not meant to be a prison, 139
what would it profit us to win the whole, 73

world organization, the troubles of a, merely reflect the troubles of the world itself, 136

world problem, there cannot be an American solution to every, 33

worship, freedom of, has brought people to America, 121

wrongs for which there are no remedies at law, 100
working to right the, 62

Y

youth, We need to strengthen our nation by investing in our, 56